CULTURAL
INTELLIGENCE

Living and Working Globally
SECOND EDITION

DAVID C. THOMAS

and

KERR INKSON

BK

Berrett–Koehler Publishers, Inc.
San Francisco
a BK Business book

Berrett-Koehler Publishers, Inc.
1333 Broadway, Suite 1000
Oakland, CA 94612-1921
Tel: (510) 817-2277   Fax: (510) 817-2278
www.bkconnection.com

Ordering Information

Quantity sales. Special discounts are available on quantity purchases by corporations, associations, and others. For details, contact the "Special Sales Department" at the Berrett-Koehler address above.

Individual sales. Berrett-Koehler publications are available through most bookstores. They can also be ordered directly from Berrett-Koehler: Tel: (800) 929-2929; Fax: (802) 864-7626; www.bkconnection.com

Orders for college textbook/course adoption use. Please contact Berrett-Koehler: Tel: (800) 929-2929; Fax: (802) 864-7626.

Orders by U.S. trade bookstores and wholesalers. Please contact Ingram Publisher Services, Tel: (800) 509-4887; Fax: (800) 838-1149; E-mail: customer.service@ingrampublisherservices.com; or visit www.ingrampublisherservices.com/Ordering for details about electronic ordering.

Berrett-Koehler and the BK logo are registered trademarks of Berrett-Koehler Publishers, Inc.

Printed in the United States of America

Berrett-Koehler books are printed on long-lasting acid-free paper. When it is available, we choose paper that has been manufactured by environmentally responsible processes. These may include using trees grown in sustainable forests, incorporating recycled paper, minimizing chlorine in bleaching, or recycling the energy produced at the paper mill.

Library of Congress Cataloging-in-Publication Data

Thomas, David C., (David Clinton), 1947–
    Cultural intelligence : living and working globally / David C. Thomas and Kerr Inkson. — 2nd ed.
        p. cm.
    Includes bibliographical references and index.
    ISBN 978-1-57675-625-6 (alk. paper)
        1. Intercultural communication. 2. Cultural awareness. 3. Cross-cultural orientation. I. Inkson, Kerr. II. Title.
    HM1211.T486   2009
    302.3'5—dc22   2009011741

SECOND EDITION
20   19   18   17   16   15   10   9   8   7   6

Project management and design: BookMatters, Berkeley; copyediting: Mike Mollett; proofing: Anne Smith; indexing: Leonard Rosenbaum.

Cultural Intelligence

To Tilley:
Whose support and affection can
only be explained by the fact that
she finds obsessive-compulsive
behavior attractive in some way.
— Dave

To Nan:
Whose love always supports me,
and sometimes inspires me, in my
writing and everything else I do.
— Kerr

Contents

Preface

This book is an update of our first book on cultural intelligence, the basis of the people skills that are critical to management success in today's global environment. In this second edition we apply these concepts more broadly to the interactions of people not just in organizations but more broadly in their daily lives.

In October 2008, as we—Kerr in Auckland, New Zealand, and Dave in Vancouver, Canada—were working on the final draft of this edition, we were once again reminded of the forces of globalization that are shaping the environment in which we must all learn to function. The global nature of the financial crisis that began with subprime mortgages in the United States but resonated around the world made the degree of integration of the economies in the world fairly obvious. Globalization has many effects, but one of the most important is the dramatic increase in the opportunity and need to interact with people who are culturally different from ourselves.

Both of us live in very multicultural cities and are reminded in our daily lives of the tremendous variety of attitudes, values, beliefs, and assumptions about appropriate behavior that culturally different individuals hold. Yet in order to solve the problems of today's global society, indeed in order to function day to day, we must learn to understand and integrate these differences. The range of cultures we encounter may be slightly unusual, but only slightly as migration patterns respond to rapid economic and political changes occurring around the world. The world is becoming more interdependent; to keep pace we must all learn to think globally—we must all develop our *cultural intelligence!*

This book is about becoming more effective in dealing with people from different cultural backgrounds. It is about acquiring the global people skills that are important for functioning in the twenty-first century and beyond. It is for people who travel overseas and encounter new cultures, as well as for those who stay at home and find that other cultures have come to them. It is about acquiring the *cultural intelligence* in order not only to survive without difficulty or embarrassment in our new multicultural environment but also to pursue our goals in this environment with the confidence needed for success.

Like its predecessor, this book is different from many other books you may have seen about cross-cultural skills or living and working in other countries.

First, this book is not country-specific. We do not provide laundry lists of drills and routines that should be applied in this country or that. Our intent is rather to help you to acquire a way of thinking and being that can be applied to any number of countries and cultures.

Second, this book is based on years of sound academic research. However, it is not an academic text, and we have tried to present important concepts in a straightforward way. To make the learning concrete, we have illustrated each chapter with a number of case studies in cross-cultural behavior, from various cultural settings.

Finally, we don't promise that this book will solve all your interpersonal problems, either at work or in your daily life.

However, we sincerely believe that if you read and apply the concepts outlined here, you will be well on your way to acquiring a critical contemporary skill—cultural intelligence.

Cultural intelligence builds on earlier concepts that you have probably heard of: the intelligence quotient (IQ) and emotional intelligence (EQ), the idea that it is important how we handle our emotions. Cultural intelligence (CQ) incorporates the capability to interact effectively across cultures. The concept is easy to understand, but it takes time and effort to develop high levels of cultural intelligence. However, becoming culturally intelligent is essentially learning by doing and has useful outcomes beyond the development of skilled intercultural performance. In addition, different cultures are fascinating, and learning them can be a lot of fun. This book is the place to start the journey.

The first three chapters outline the fundamentals of cultural intelligence. Chapter 1 shows how a lack of cultural intelligence can negatively affect intercultural interactions. It examines the problems with current methods of addressing these cross-cultural issues and identifies acquiring cultural intelligence as a more productive approach. The next two chapters outline the principles and practice of cultural intelligence. Chapter 2 helps you to *understand* what cultural differences are and how they are reflected in different people's behavior. Chapter 3 helps you to *discard your assumptions* about the way people "should" behave, practice *mindfulness*—a kind of attention to culturally based behavior—and develop *skills* for use in cross-cultural situations. The message in these chapters is that the task of understanding culture is difficult but not impossible, and if you learn the basic principles, adopt a mindful approach, and are prepared to act as a culturally adaptive person, you can function effectively in a variety of cross-cultural settings. Moreover, it will be a rewarding experience for you.

The next four chapters apply the fundamentals of cultural intelligence to a number of common interpersonal challenges in multicultural settings. By applying the principles outlined, you can be more effective in making decisions (chapter 4); communicating, negotiating, and resolving conflicts across cultures (chapter 5); leading and motivating others who are culturally different (chapter 6); and designing, managing, and contributing to multicultural groups and teams (chapter 7). In chapter 8 you will learn how cross-cultural understanding, mindfulness, and skills are acquired and can be developed by means of education, everyday experience, and foreign travel. Finally, we provide a bibliography of key sources for those wanting to explore cultural intelligence in more depth.

Kerr is a Scot who lives and works in New Zealand. Dave is a New Zealand citizen but was born and educated in the United States and now lives and works in Canada. As we write and teach about cultural diversity, we are constantly reminded of our own cultural backgrounds. While we both have extensive international experience and between us have lived and worked in ten different countries, we know that these backgrounds influence how we think and write. We have worked very hard to be objective in this regard, but we would be pleased to hear from readers who feel we have missed or misinterpreted things that are obvious to them from their cultural perspective.

With this book we have attempted to help readers understand and integrate cultural differences, to appreciate the wonderful diversity of our fellow human beings all around the world, and to help people everywhere become more knowledgeable, more attentive, and more skilled in their interactions with others. We sincerely believe that by developing cultural intelligence, we can all make the world a more productive and a happier place.

Dave Thomas
Vancouver

Kerr Inkson
Auckland

Acknowledgments

Numerous individuals, organizations and environments have contributed to the production of this second edition. We are grateful to Steve Piersanti at Berrett-Koehler for taking the risk of publishing our first edition, and for convincing us to make room in our schedules to do a second. Working with Jeevan Sivasubramaniam, Managing Editor, and the outstanding staff at Berrett-Koehler has made this project a pleasure. We thank Rick Wilson, Dianne Platner, and everyone at BK for caring about our books and making them the best they can be. Our thanks also go to David Peattie and his colleagues at BookMatters for their efforts in making our book pleasing to look at and easy to read and to Mike Mollett, who has worked on both editions of the book, this time as copyeditor. We are also grateful to Christopher Morris, Joseph Webb, and Danielle Scott for their helpful reviews of the first edition and our plans for a revision. We also thank Peter Heslin for his comments on the feedback he received from students for whom he prescribed our first edition. Any errors and omissions are of course our responsibility alone.

Positive comments about the first edition from readers and colleagues also inspired us to proceed with this volume. Many of the ideas in this book were the product of, or refined in, numerous discussions that Dave has had with members of the International Organization Network (ION). We are grateful to Richard Brislin for many of the examples of cross-cultural interactions that we have adapted for use here and to Andre Pekerti for culture-specific advice. Yuan Liao reviewed many of our Chinese examples and provided research assistance. Thank you, Echo!

Our work on this book has paralleled work by the Cultural Intelligence Project, which has been developing a vehicle for assessing cultural intelligence. Led by Dave, this international consortium is doing work that both inspires and informs this book. Members of the Cultural Intelligence Project are Kevin Au, Zeynep Aycan, Richard Brislin, Jean-Luc Cerdin, Bjørn Ekelund, Efrat Elron, Mila Lazarova, Martha Maznevski, Andre Pekerti, Steven Poelmans, Elizabeth Ravlin, and Günter Stahl.

This volume is informed not only by our academic study but by the numerous cross-cultural encounters that make culture come alive for us. Therefore, we thank all those people who have helped to educate us and beg forgiveness from those we have offended along the way through our own lack of cultural intelligence.

CHAPTER 1

Living and Working in the Global Village

Bob Weber hangs up the telephone and leaps to his feet. Furious, he bounds out of his office in search of his Korean-born administrative assistant, Joanne Park. He has just been berated by his customer in Pennsylvania for not sending the contract for softwood lumber to him on the date specified. This exchange, plus the current volatility in the Canadian stock market, is really making him edgy. As he walks down the hall toward the employee lunchroom, he begins to calm down. He knows he must handle this situation with an employee carefully.

He arrives at the lunchroom and pokes his head in the door.

"Is Joanne here?" He sees her at a table, sharing her lunch with several other administrative staff. He still feels annoyed, but he keeps his voice in control.

"Oh, I see you are in here. I was looking for that contract to Zott Industries that I asked you to type. Did you forget?"

Everyone stops talking. They look uncomfortable. Joanne gets up from the table.

"Oh, Mr. Weber. I am so sorry! I will do it right this minute!"

"No, that's okay. After lunch is fine. But, we do need to get it out today." He goes out.

1

Joanne averts her eyes. She looks miserable. The other staff are looking at each other knowingly.

A few minutes later Bob is sitting behind his desk busily talking on the telephone. Joanne comes in briskly and delivers the contract (with two hands, typical of Korean culture) into Bob's in-box.

She then turns and goes out just as briskly and closes the door firmly but quietly behind her.

Bob ends his phone call, gets up from his desk, and follows Joanne into the hall. His anger has gone. After all, Joanne has never made such a mistake before. Now he is concerned for her.

"Joanne, can you come in here for a minute."

Joanne comes in obediently and stands in front of him with her head down, not making eye contact with Bob.

"Is there some sort of a problem here? If so, we need to talk about it."

There is no response from Joanne.

"Does it have something to do with forgetting to type the contract?"

Joanne nods. She still doesn't look at him.

He is conciliatory, friendly. "Oh! That was no big deal! It's done now. Just forget about it. But in the future just make sure and tell me if something is wrong so we can talk it out. Okay?"

Joanne nods again.

Over the next few weeks Joanne takes several days of sick leave, and three weeks later she resigns.

The actions and reactions of Bob Weber and Joanne Park reveal quite different outlooks on resolving a problem at the office. Like most Americans, Bob thinks the best way to resolve conflicts is to have a frank and open discussion about them and work through any differences. In contrast, Joanne's cultural background tells her that she will never be able to recover the status she had formerly enjoyed after being reprimanded in front of her peers. And being confronted again with her mistake by Bob in his office just added to her loss of face. Both Bob and Joanne continue to operate as if they were totally immersed among others of their own culture.

As a result, both Bob and Joanne endanger the things they value most: Bob, despite his good intentions, has failed to correct the cause of the administrative error and portray himself as a caring boss. And Joanne has left a job in a good organization that she generally enjoyed. If each had been willing and able to accommodate, at least in part, the other's customs and had made more effort to help the other to understand his or her own customs, Bob might have been able to create an efficient and friendly working environment, and Joanne might have learned some new ways of dealing with her new culture.

For example, Bob might have had some discussions with the other managers who have Korean staff and adjusted some of his managerial style and communication behavior. For her part, Joanne might have noted her own feelings and communicated to Bob how his behavior affected her.

The story of Bob Weber and Joanne Park is typical—it is a story that is enacted again and again in many situations around the world as ordinary people, working both within their own countries and overseas, grapple with the problem of relating to others who are from cultures where things are done differently.

Consider the following examples:

- A British company trying to run a Japanese subsidiary experiences inexplicable problems of morale and conflict with its Japanese workforce. This seems out of character with the usual politeness and teamwork of the Japanese. Later it is found that the British manager of the operation in Japan is not taken seriously because she is a woman.

- Two American managers meet with executives and engineers of a large Chinese electronics firm to present their idea for a joint venture. After several meetings, they notice that different engineers seem to be attending the meetings and that their questions are becoming more technical, so much so that the Americans have difficulty answering them without giving away trade secrets. The Americans think this attempt to gain technological information is ridiculous. Don't the Chinese have any business ethics? How do they sleep at night? Later they learn that this is common practice and considered to be good business among the Chinese, who often suspect that westerners are interested only in exploiting a cheap labor market.

- In Malaysia, an old woman is struggling to unload some furniture from a cart and carry it into her house. The furniture is heavy, and she stumbles under the weight. Many people crowd the street, but no one makes an effort to offer help. A couple of young American tourists who are passing by see the problem, rush up, and start helping the old lady. The locals on the street seem bemused and perplexed by these Americans helping someone they don't even know.

- A Canadian manager faces difficulties because his five key subordinates are, respectively, French-Canadian, Indian, Italian-American, Chinese, and Iraqi. How can he treat them equitably? How can he find a managerial style that works with all of them? How should he chair meetings?

- A Dutch couple, an engineer and a teacher who have volunteered for two-year assignments in Sri Lanka to assist local economic development, spend an evening visiting a Sri Lankan couple to whom they have been introduced by a friend. They want to "get a feel for" the Sri Lankan people. Their hosts are gracious and hospitable but much more reserved than the Dutch couple are used to. The guests feel awkward and find it hard to make conversation. Later, they panic because of the ineptitude they felt in dealing with the Sri Lankans.[1]

These stories provide real-life examples of people from different parts of the world struggling with problems caused by intercultural differences. Do you identify with any of these situations? Do you wonder how to deal with people from other countries, cultures, or ethnic groups? Have you been in situations, like the ones above, that have left you puzzled and frustrated because you simply haven't felt tuned in to the people you have been dealing with? If so, you are not alone; you are attempting to operate in a multicultural world.

The Global Village

There are seven billion people in the world from myriad different cultures, but we live in a village where events taking place ten thousand miles away seem as close as events happening in the next street. We find ourselves in this global village whenever we read a newspaper or watch television or buy a product from the grocery store shelf. We can watch a Middle East firefight as if we were there, eat tropical fruit with snow on the ground outside, and meet people from far-off exotic places at the local mall. The following dramatic examples of globalization are familiar to almost everyone.

THE GLOBAL WORLD COMES TO THE UNITED STATES

Americans' consciousness of the increasingly global society that they live in has been powerfully raised by what may turn out to be the two major crises of the first decade of the new millennium.

On September 11, 2001, the world came to America in a new and horrifying way. The young men who flew their hijacked airliners into the great U.S. citadels of the World Trade Center and the Pentagon were citizens of the global village. They were operating in a world with a profoundly increased consciousness of difference—haves versus have-nots, Christians versus Muslims—as well as far fewer boundaries. To the terrorists, America was not a distant vision but an outrage beamed nightly into their homes through their televisions, a place they could visit personally for the price of a plane ticket. They slipped easily into the world's most powerful nation, acquired its language, were accepted by their neighbors, and took flying lessons from friendly, helpful locals. Most likely they tuned in to U.S. television at night and paid special attention to the regular bulletins on conflict in the Middle East.

The news of the attacks traveled, virtually instantaneously, to all corners of the world. Californians stared aghast at the strange horrors of the day's breakfast show. Europeans interrupted their shopping to crowd around television screens in appliance store windows. Australians phoned each other in the night and said, "Switch your telly on." A billion viewers around the globe watched as the Twin Towers collapsed in front of their eyes.

After September 11, people struggled to understand. Who were these people who had plunged the world into crisis? Where were they from? What did they believe? What was it in the ever more complicated cause-and-effect kaleidoscope of global economics and politics that America had done to cause such bitter enmity among these terrorists and their supporters?

In October 2008 people around the world again watched in horror as the financial morass labeled by the term *subprime mortgages* quickly spread into their lives. Some of the biggest and apparently most impregnable financial institutions suddenly went out of business, crippled by multibillion-dollar debts. Flows of credit—the lifeblood of business—froze, stock markets plunged, and memories of the horrors of the Great Depression of the 1930s were revived. The president of the United States quickly called his top advisers together to put together a rescue package, and within a few days a $700 billion government "bailout" of stricken banks was announced—a de facto reversal of the country's most cherished principles of free-market capitalism.

Despite this intervention, however, the share markets continued to fall. And they fell not just in the United States but all around the world. Banks in many countries had to be bailed out by their governments. It seemed that the "toxic mortgages" that had started the problem had ended up being processed into various forms of "derivative" debt and exported all around the world. In addition, it turned out that the culture of lax bank regulation and incentivization of massive, unsustainable credit was not a particularly American problem but one shared and developed in concert with many other industrialized countries. So it was only when the world's leaders *all* came together, in meetings of the G7 and G20 countries (meetings of the leading industrialized counties), and developed integrated *global* solutions to a global problem, that the bleeding stopped and markets around the world begun to stabilize. At the end of 2008, it was not just America but all countries that faced bleak economic times ahead.

After both of these events, people said, "The world will never be the same again." What they might rather have said: "The world has been changing rapidly for some time. These events have caused us to notice it."

These events can be understood only if one takes a global perspective. These matters are not just about New York or about America or about the Middle East and its relationship with America or about finance in the developed world. The forces involved are economic, political, legal, and cultural forces that cross international boundaries, create international problems, and require international solutions. We all see these things, and whether we like it or not, we are all involved. We are all citizens in a global world. And none of us can escape the fact.

Forces of Globalization

We are all living increasingly global lives. And we are beginning to see and understand the importance of the process known as globalization, particularly the way it affects the lives of people. Globalization means an increase in the permeability of traditional boundaries, not just those around business organizations but those around countries, economies, industries, and people.[2]

Globalization has accelerated by a host of factors in the international business environment, including the following:

- Increased international interconnectedness, as represented by trade agreements, the growth of international trade, the growth of multinational corporations, and the ability to locate business, particularly manufacturing, wherever cost is lowest.

- The increased volume and importance of human migration, particularly from less-developed to more-developed countries. In many nations now a large percentage of inhabitants were born and brought up in other countries or are culturally influenced by their parents who were themselves immigrants.

- The ability of information and communication technology to transcend time and distance so that at the touch of a computer keyboard or a cell phone, we can be somewhere else, thousands of kilometers away, and participate in events and change outcomes there.

Until recently only a few very large multinational companies were concerned with foreign operations. Now, business extends across all manner of porous boundaries—some of which have become so porous they have almost ceased to exist—across the entire globe. Even very small firms now have the capability to be global: indeed, small and medium-sized organizations account for an ever-increasing share of global business.

Because of globalization, the environment of business is now more complex, more dynamic, more uncertain, and more competitive than ever before. And there is no evidence that these trends will reverse or decrease. Tomorrow's managers, even more than today's, will have to learn to compete, and to work, in a global world.

Globalization of People

However, globalization affects not only businesses and their managers but employees at all levels, as well as customers and indeed everyone in the general population. Inevitably, globalization brings about interactions and relationships between people who are culturally different. In business today, and as tourists and members of families, networks, and communities that have "gone international," we travel overseas among people from other cultures, we speak with them on international telephone calls, and we correspond with them by e-mail. Even in our home cities, we notice that more and more of our colleagues, our clients, and even the people we pass in the street are observably from cultures different from our own. The trend is inexorable. This globalization of people creates a new and major challenge for everyone, especially those who work in business. Although we increasingly cross boundaries and surmount barriers to trade, migration, travel, and the exchange of information, cultural boundaries are not so easily bridged. Unlike legal, political, or economic aspects of the global environment, which are observable, culture is largely invisible. Therefore, culture is the aspect of the global context that is most often overlooked.

The potential problems are enormous. Even when people come from the same culture, interpersonal skills are often poor, and this weakness is costly to business. Where interpersonal interaction is taking place across cultural boundaries, the potential for misunderstanding and failure is compounded.

The conclusion is clear. Whether you are conscious of it or not, you are a member of the global community. This is true, even if you have never done business abroad or even traveled abroad. You may never have gone around the globe, but the globe has come to you. Any organization you work for will most likely buy or sell in another country, or will at least be influenced by global events. And you will increasingly have to interact with people from all parts of the globe right in your own home town.

Here is a story about two global people. One is an international migrant who is trying to create a new environment for himself in a very different place. The other is a manager who has never left her own country but now is confronted by an immigrant from a part of the globe she has never been to, coming into her office and sitting down in front of her.

THE JOB APPLICANT

In California, the human resource manager of a manufacturing company sits in her office. She is interviewing candidates for factory work, and the next candidate is due. Suddenly the door opens, and a dark-skinned young man walks in without knocking. He does not look at the manager but walks to the nearest chair and, without waiting to be invited, sits down. He makes no eye contact with the manager but instead stares at the floor. The manager is appalled at such graceless behavior. Can't the man even say "Good morning"? The interview has not even started, and even though the jobs being filled do not require strong social skills, it is already unlikely that the young man will be appointed.

Observing this scene, most Americans and Western Europeans might think that the human resource manager has come too quickly to a conclusion about a candidate who may have the potential to be a good worker, but they would fully understand why she felt as she did. The man's behavior certainly seems odd and disrespectful.

But suppose we give the manager some new knowledge about the young man and his perspective on the interaction.

The young man is Samoan. He was born and brought up in Samoa and only recently immigrated to the United States. Samoans have great respect for authority, and the young man sees the manager as an important authority figure, deserving of considerable respect. In Samoa you do not speak to, or even make eye contact with, authority figures until they invite you to do so. You do not stand while they are sitting, because to do so would put you on a physically higher level than they are, implying serious disrespect. In other words, in terms of his own cultural background and training, the young man has behaved exactly as he should. The human resource manager in this case, if she herself were a job candidate, would greet her interviewer politely, make eye contact, offer a handshake, and wait to be invited to sit down. Therefore, she tends to expect similar behavior of everyone she interviews. In doing so, she is not only being unfair to candidates who for various reasons operate differently, she is also reducing her (and her company's) opportunity to benefit and learn from people from different cultural backgrounds.

We are all different, yet all too often we expect everyone else to be like us. If they don't do things the way we would do them, we assume something is wrong with them. Why can't we think outside our little cultural rule books, accept and enjoy the wonderful diversity of humankind, and learn to work in harmony with others' ways?

In the cases we have provided so far, Bob Weber and Joanne Park and the human resource manager and the young Samoan man are playing a game that we all play. The game is called *Be Like Me*. Do it *my* way. Follow *my* rules. And, when the other party can't, or doesn't want to, the characters in our stories withdraw into baffled incomprehension.

We all tend to be like Bob and Joanne and the human resource manager and the young Samoan man. We all find cultural differences hard to deal with. We all tend to play *Be Like Me* with the people we live and work with.

Intercultural Failures

Many of us fail in intercultural situations is in all sorts of ways, such as the following:

- Being unaware of the key features and biases of our own culture. Remember that just as other cultures may seem odd to us, ours is odd to people from other cultures. For example, few Americans realize how noisy their natural extroversion and manner of conversation seem to those from most other cultures, many of which value reticence and modesty. By the same token, people from Asian societies, where long silences in conversations are considered normal and acceptable as participants reflect on the topic, do not realize how odd and intimidating silence in this situation seems to many Westerners.

- Feeling threatened or uneasy when interacting with people who are culturally different. We may work not to be prejudiced against people from other cultures, but we notice, usually with tiny internal feelings of apprehension, the physical characteristics of others that make them different from us. All of us find difference threatening to some extent.

- Being unable to understand or explain the behavior of others who are culturally different. When we use a *Be Like Me* approach to explaining the behavior of others, we are often wrong, because their behavior may not be based on the same goals or motives as ours.

- Being unable to transfer knowledge about one culture to another culture. Even people who have lots of travel experience in many different countries are often unable to use this experience to be more effective in each subsequent intercultural encounter.

- Not recognizing when our own cultural orientation is influencing our behavior. Much of our behavior is programmed by culture at a very deep level of consciousness, and we are often unaware of this influence. Behavior that is normal to us may seem abnormal or even bizarre to culturally different others.

- Being unable to adjust to living and working in another culture. Anyone who has lived in a foreign culture for six months or more can attest to the difficulty in adjustment. The severity of culture shock may vary, but it affects us all.

- Being unable to develop long-term interpersonal relationships with people from other cultures, because even if we learn how to understand them and communicate with them a little better, the effort of doing so puts us off trying to develop the relationships any further.

In all of these examples, stress and anxiety for all parties is increased, and the end result is often impaired performance, loss of potential satisfaction and personal growth, and, in organizations, lost business opportunities.

Ways of Overcoming Cultural Difference

If the above are the symptoms, what is the cure? How can we ordinary people acquire the ability to feel at home when dealing with those from other cultures, to know what to say and do, and to pursue business and other relationships with the same degree of relaxation and the same expectation of synergy and success that we experience in relationships with people from our own culture?

EXPECTING OTHERS TO ADAPT

One way of trying to deal with the problem is to stick to the *Be Like Me* policy and try to brazen it out. We can reason, particularly if we come from a dominating economy or culture such as the United States, that it is for us to set norms for behavior and for others to learn how to imitate us.

You may think there is something in this. First, a dominant culture may win in the end anyway.[3] For example, the English language is becoming the lingua franca of business and education, and is increasingly spoken in business and professional interactions all over Europe and large parts of Asia. Second, many people believe that different cultures are converging to a common norm, assisted by phenomena such as mass communication and the "McDonaldization" of consumption.[4] Eventually, they argue, the whole world will become like the United States anyway, and its citizens will think, talk, and act like people from the United States. Many cities around the world already mimic New York, with the same organizations, brands, and architectural and dress styles; why resist the process?

In fact, the evidence in favor of cultural convergence is

not compelling. Convergence is probably taking place only in superficial matters such as business procedures and consumer preferences.[5] Also, insisting that other people behave as we do robs us of the great gift of diversity and the novelty it brings in the form of new ways of thinking and working. Finally, anyone who plays *Be Like Me* overtly or excessively is behaving insensitively and will be perceived as insensitive by others. Under these circumstances, many opportunities will soon disappear.

UNDERSTANDING CULTURAL DIFFERENCES

Can we solve the problem of cultural differences and seize the opportunity they create simply by learning what other cultures are like? Do we even know, in any organized way, what they are like?

Plenty of easily accessible information about other cultures is available. Cultural anthropologists have researched many of the cultures of the world, and cultural differences affecting specific fields such as education, health, and business have also been explored.[6] This information has been useful in establishing the behavior or cultural stereotypes of many national cultures, and it provides a starting point for anticipating culturally based behavior.

Understanding some of the key cultural differences between countries and how those differences affect behavior is an important first step on the way to gaining cultural intelligence. This book provides some basic information on these matters.

However, this basic knowledge is only the beginning of the process of changing cultural differences from a handicap to an asset. Even at their best, research on cultural difference and the sort of account that says, "Japanese behave in this way and Americans in that" can provide only a broad statement about cultural identity. Generalizations about a country are likely to conceal huge variances within that country and considerable subtlety in the way cultural differences are made apparent. A country may have, for example, religious or tribal or ethnic differences, forms of special protocol, or regional variations.

The "laundry-list" approach to cross-cultural understanding attempts to provide each individual who is to have intercultural interactions with a list—"everything you need to know"—about the particular country. Such lists often attempt to detail not just what the key cultural characteristics of the country are but the regional or organizational variations, the expected behavior in that country, the detailed customs to be followed, the type of speech inflections to use, and expressions and actions that might be considered offensive, as well as functional information on matters such as living costs, health services, and education. Tourists and travelers can buy books of this type about most countries, and some companies preparing executives for an assignment to a foreign country take this approach to preparing prospective assignees and their families for the transition.

Laundry lists have their place, but they are cumbersome. They have to document every trait of every conceivable cultural variant, along with drills and routines to cater for each. For an expatriate, this kind of intensive preparation for a single destination may be highly appropriate, but for most of us our engagement with other cultures is a less intensive interaction with a variety of cultures. If we are traveling in, or entertaining visitors or interacting with immigrants from half a dozen countries, do we have to learn an elaborate laundry list for each one? If we are suddenly introduced to culturally different people without warning and have no laundry list readily available, how can we cope with the situation?

Furthermore, laundry lists tend to be rather dry and formal. The essence of culture is subtler, it is expressed in combination with the unique personality of each individual, and it is hard to express in print. Formal and abstract knowledge needs to be supplemented by and integrated with experience of the culture and interactions with its people. Learning facts about other cultures is not enough.

A third approach to the problem is to become culturally intelligent.[7]

Cultural intelligence means being skilled and flexible about understanding a culture, learning more about it from your ongoing interactions with it, and gradually reshaping your thinking to be more sympathetic to the culture and developing your behavior to be more skilled and appropriate when interacting with others from the culture. We must learn to be flexible enough to adapt to each new cultural situation that we face with knowledge and sensitivity.

Cultural intelligence consists of three parts.

- First, the culturally intelligent person requires *knowledge* of culture and of the fundamental principles of cross-cultural interactions. This means knowing what culture is, how cultures vary, and how culture affects behavior.

- Second, the culturally intelligent person needs to practice *mindfulness,* the ability to pay attention in a reflective and creative way to cues in the cross-cultural situations encountered and to one's own knowledge and feelings.

- Third, based on knowledge and mindfulness, the culturally intelligent person develops cross-cultural *skills* and becomes competent across a wide range of situations. These skills involve choosing the appropriate behavior from a well-developed repertoire of behaviors that are correct for different intercultural situations.

The model in figure 1.1 is a graphic representation of cultural intelligence.

Each element in figure 1.1 is interrelated with the others. As we describe in chapter 8, the process of becoming culturally intelligent involves a cycle or repetition in which each new challenge builds upon previous ones until cultural intelligence is ultimately achieved. A major advantage of this approach

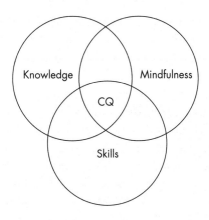

FIGURE 1.1. Components of cultural intelligence (CQ)

over the laundry-list approach is that as well as acquiring growing competence in a specific culture you simultaneously acquire general cultural intelligence, making each new cultural challenge easier to face because of what has been learned from the previous ones.

You have probably heard of the psychologists' concept of intelligence, the ability to reason, and its measure, the intelligence quotient (IQ). More recently has come recognition of emotional intelligence, the concept that it is important how we handle our emotions. A measure of emotional intelligence is the emotional intelligence quotient (EQ). Cultural intelligence (or CQ as its measure might be called) is a relatively new idea that builds on these earlier concepts but that incorporates the capability to interact effectively across cultures.[8]

In the three chapters that follow, we present a road map for improving your cultural intelligence by addressing the three elements of cultural intelligence one by one.

In chapter 2 we examine the information base that provides the necessary background understanding of cultural phenomena. A secure *knowledge* of what culture is and what it is not;

of the depth, strength, and shared and systematic nature of culture; and of some of the main types of cultural difference provides a good basic set of tools to give one confidence in any cross-cultural situation.

In chapter 3 we consider how observation of the everyday behavior of people from different backgrounds—including our own behavior—can be useful in interpreting the frameworks of knowledge introduced in chapter 2. Most people operate interpersonally in a condition of "cruise control," in which their experiences are interpreted from the standpoint of their own culture. We develop the idea of *mindfulness*—a process of observing and reflecting that incorporates cross-cultural knowledge. Developing the habit and the techniques of mindfulness is a key means to improving cultural intelligence. We then outline the process through which knowledge and mindfulness lead to new skilled behavior. The *cross-cultural skills* associated with cultural intelligence are general skills that are derived from specific knowledge. By developing this repertoire of behavior, you can translate the understanding of culture into effective cross-cultural interactions. Finally in chapter 4 we show how you can develop a functioning cultural intelligence.

The concept of cultural intelligence as outlined in this book is not difficult to understand, but is hard to put into practice on an ongoing basis. It takes time and effort to develop a high CQ and the accompanying skills. Years of studying, observing, reflecting, and experimenting likely lie ahead before the learner develops truly skilled performance. Becoming culturally intelligent is substantially learning by doing, so it has useful outcomes beyond the development of skilled intercultural performance. In addition, new cultures are intriguing: learning how to live in them or work in them or interact with people who are from them can be fun and can open up wonderful possibilities of new insights, new relationships, and a new richness in your life. This book is the place to start on this journey.

Summary

This chapter describes the forces of globalization that are dramatically changing the environment for people around the globe. Those confronted by the phenomenon of cultural difference and diversity include not just global managers but all of us. In a sense we are all becoming global managers, for even those who stay in their own countries have to think in global terms. The essence of being global is interacting with people who are culturally different from ourselves. Culture is more difficult to deal with than other aspects of the environment, partly because much of culture operates invisibly. We know a great deal about how cultures around the world differ. However, this knowledge is only the beginning of the process of becoming culturally intelligent. Cultural intelligence involves understanding the fundamentals of intercultural interaction, developing a mindful approach to intercultural interactions, and finally building cross-cultural skills and a repertoire of behaviors so that one can be effective in any intercultural situation. Interacting effectively across cultures is now a fundamental requirement for all of us in today's global environment.

CHAPTER 2

Cultural Knowledge

WE CAN MAKE THE BEST OF IT

Chan Yuk Fai ushered his British guest into the crowded Shanghai restaurant. Around them, the atmosphere was busy with the quiet babble of a dozen conversations. Mr. Chan bowed slightly, then leaned forward and smiled. "I think," he said in excellent English, "I think the food is not the very best in this restaurant."

Jeffrey Thomson stiffened slightly. He found it hard to conceal his surprise. What was he to make of Mr. Chan's remark? Mr. Chan had chosen the restaurant. Did he really think the food was poor? If he thought so, why had be chosen this restaurant? Perhaps criticizing the food was just a Chinese custom—something everyone did that had nothing to do with the real quality of the food. Perhaps it was a joke—Mr. Chan was smiling broadly. After all, what did Jeffrey know about the Chinese sense of humor? Or perhaps it was an affectation of modesty. He had read somewhere that Chinese were self-effacing. But he had also read that they were indirect. Maybe criticizing the restaurant was Mr. Chan's way of saying he did not have a lot of interest in Jeffrey or what he had to say. Maybe it was even some form of veiled insult!

He realized that Mr. Chan was politely waiting for him to respond and that he had no idea what to say. He felt very confused.

Best to be noncommittal, he thought. What would I say if someone said that to me in London? He smiled back at Mr. Chan. "I'm sure we can make the best of it," he replied.

Was it his imagination, or did he see a minuscule reduction in Mr. Chan's beaming smile?[1]

On the surface Jeffrey Thomson's worries about Chinese culture have to do with Chinese customs, the habitual ways in which people go about day-to-day activities. The Chinese custom is to show respect for a guest by disparaging one's own accomplishments, even the selection of a restaurant. And the expectation is that the guest will return this respect with a compliment. By not doing so, Jeffrey has made a cultural blunder. This custom is specific to the cultural situation, but the general predicament in which Jeffrey finds himself is one that he has in common with thousands of other travelers from all continents and countries. Jeffrey *does* have some understanding of the notion that important cultural differences exist between himself and Mr. Chan. There is some truth in his inner reflections on Chinese people tending to be self-effacing and inscrutable. And he is trying to use his powers of observation to draw an appropriate conclusion and behave in an appropriate way. But his knowledge, his insight, and his experience are simply insufficient for the task. He lacks cultural intelligence.

Components of Cultural Intelligence

Jeffrey's problem can be divided into three linked components.

First, he lacks detailed *knowledge*. He understands that there are such things as cross-cultural differences. His mind has retained a few ideas (from where, who knows?) about characteristics of Chinese people like the man he is dealing with. But these are crude stereotypes that leave open multiple interpretations and are of little help in enabling him to understand the situation.

Second, he lacks *mindfulness*. Not only does he not know what Mr. Chan's remark means, but he lacks the ability to observe and interpret the remark in the context of other cues—prior conversations, his dealings with other Chinese, the visible quality of the restaurant he is standing in, Mr. Chan's smile, and so on. Because of this, he is unable to read the situation as it develops. Whatever the outcome, he is likely to learn little from the experience that will assist him with further interactions. Mindfulness is a means of continually observing and understanding cultural meanings and using that understanding as a basis for immediate action and long-term learning.

Third, he lacks the *skill* to adapt his behavior. He would love to be able to respond confidently, in both his words and his physical actions, in a way that would be authentic but also sensitive to his host. He realizes that being able to respond appropriately to Mr. Chan's remark would not only put both of them more at ease but would also help their conversation. But the only action he is capable of—because of his lack of both knowledge and interpretive skills—is to respond as he would "at home." Jeffrey needs to develop a repertoire of behaviors that will enable him to act appropriately and successfully in any cross-cultural situation.

The three components combined provide a template for intercultural flexibility and competence. In brief, culturally intelligent people have:

- the *knowledge* to understand cross-cultural phenomena
- the *mindfulness* to observe and interpret particular situations
- the *skills* required to adapt *behavior* to act appropriately and successfully in a range of situations

These three components are connected to each other and build on each other. Because culturally intelligent people have good background understanding, their interpretation is assisted—they know what to look for. But each competency is also based on wider characteristics that we all have to different degrees: those who find cultural intelligence easiest to acquire are people who are interested in novel learning and social interaction and who already have good communication skills. For those who are unsure of themselves in these areas, acquiring cultural intelligence is also likely to increase competence and confidence in *all* interpersonal situations.[2]

In this chapter we focus on the information base—or *knowledge*—that is the first component of cultural intelligence. In the case study, a culturally intelligent Jeffrey would have been mindfully aware of Mr. Chan's remarks and would have adapted his behavior by choosing from a number of more appropriate responses. But in order to do this Jeffrey would have needed a basic understanding of culture.

What Culture Is

Culture is a word that is familiar to everyone, but its precise meaning can be elusive. A useful definition by noted social scientist Geert Hofstede is that culture consists of shared mental programs that condition individuals' responses to their environment.[3] This simple definition neatly summarizes the idea that we see culture in everyday behavior—individuals' responses to their environment, such as Chan Yuk Fai's and Jeffrey Thomson's efforts at conversation—but that such behavior is controlled by deeply embedded mental programs. Culture is not just a set of surface behaviors; it is deeply embedded in each of us. The surface features of our social behavior—for example, our mannerisms, our ways of speaking to each other, the way we dress—are often manifestations of deep culturally based values and principles.

A key feature of culture is that these mental programs are shared—Chan Yuk Fai and Jeffrey Thomson share theirs with many other people from their own ethnic or national communities. Hofstede talks about three levels of mental programming, as shown in figure 2.1.

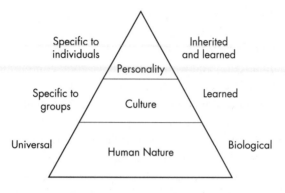

FIGURE 2.1. Three levels of mental programming

- The deepest level—*human nature*—is based on common biological reactions, such as hunger, sex drive, territoriality, and nurturing of the young, that all members of the human race have in common. Because of human nature, there are many behaviors and understandings that all people share, even though they come from different cultures.

- The shallowest level—*personality*—is based on the specific genetic makeup and personal experiences that make each of us a unique individual. For example, we may be sociable or introverted, aggressive or submissive, emotional or stable, or perhaps, as a result of learning, have a deep interest in fashionable clothing or a love of good wine. Because of personality, each of us has many behaviors and understandings that are quite different from those of others, even though they come from the same culture.

- The middle level—*culture*—is based on common experiences that we share with a particular group of our fellow human beings. Cultural values, attitudes, and assumptions about proper behavior give us something in common with a definable group of others, but not with all of them. The group may be a very large one, such as a national population, for example, Japanese culture; or a very small one, for example, the culture of the committee of a local PTA. In recent years, many business, government, and not-for-profit organizations have recognized the power of culture to shape individual values and actions and have worked hard to establish "organization cultures" that will bond the activities of diverse members to common values and themes such as customer service or conservation.[4]

In this book, we are concerned mostly with national or ethnic cultures. But the notion of smaller cultures—sometimes referred to as subcultures—and the idea of individual personality remind us that huge variation exists within any given culture and that one of the biggest barriers to effective intercultural interaction is basing our behavior on stereotypes, which assume that all members of a given culture are identical.

Characteristics of Culture

Culture has some basic characteristics that are worth keeping in mind.

CULTURE IS SHARED

By definition, culture is something that a group has in common that is not normally available to people outside the group. It is mental programming held in common that enables insiders to interact with each other with a special intimacy denied to outsiders.

For example, Scottish people all over the world share an understanding of history that is rooted in conflict with, and oppression by, the English. Even though the two groups nowadays coexist relatively harmoniously, this simple fact creates a bond among Scots and an attitude toward the English that is hard to put into words but is immediately recognized by Scottish people when they meet anywhere in the world.

CULTURE IS LEARNED AND IS ENDURING

The example of the Scots and the English tells us that culture does not arise by accident but builds up systematically over time based on sequences of historical events. The mental programming of a group is learned by its members over long periods as they interact with their environment and with each other. Some aspects of culture, such as religious beliefs, systems of land ownership, and forms of marriage, are built into institutions. Other aspects are passed on through the generations in the form of parental role modeling and advice to the young.

CULTURE IS A POWERFUL INFLUENCE ON BEHAVIOR

We have a hard time escaping our culture, even when we want to. The mental programming involved is strong. Even when we mentally question the rationality of some aspects of our culture or seek to adopt cultural flexibility by doing things in line with a different culture, we have a natural tendency to revert to our cultural roots.

For example, one young man was brought up in a strict Christian culture that taught him that the theater is the house of the devil. When he went to university and mixed with more liberal people, he decided that from a rational point of view there was nothing wrong with going to the theater. But on his first visit, he became nauseous and had to leave to be sick. His culture had programmed him extremely powerfully. To some extent this book, in encouraging cultural flexibility in cross-cultural situations, is asking readers to try to do something that may not come naturally.

Nevertheless, the experience of migrants, who deliberately and often successfully move from one cultural setting to another, suggests that individuals can learn, and even identify with, aspects of a new culture. In some cases, the requirements of a dominant culture may even cause them to suppress aspects of their original culture. These changes take place through a process known as acculturation.[5] Being embedded in an unfamiliar setting causes some to learn actively about the new culture, while others attempt to avoid it, often by trying to re-create their old culture in the new situation.[6] The best adaptation is done by those who learn the new culture while still retaining valuable elements of their original culture. By so doing, they cultivate cultural intelligence.[7]

CULTURE IS SYSTEMATIC AND ORGANIZED

Culture is not random. It is an organized system of values, attitudes, beliefs, and meanings that are related to each other and to the context. When Chan Yuk Fai says, "I think the food is not the very best in this restaurant," understanding that Chinese people often deprecate themselves is not enough. We need to understand that such deprecation is but one tiny expression of a complex system of values and ideas. It is a surface representation of Mr. Chan's deepest values and understanding of the world—a mental program based on centuries of survival and cooperation by Mr. Chan's Chinese ancestors in their largely agricultural economy and culture. As another example, the practice of polygamy, which is frowned on in most cultures, makes good historical sense in some African cultures where it is still practiced. Acceptance of polygamy depends on such factors as family status, economic security, and religious commitment, all of which are based on having more children, and particularly more sons, per family.

Because of the mental programming imposed by our own culture, the cultures of other people often seem strange and illogical. Deeper scrutiny can reveal that each culture has its own, often exquisite, logic and coherence.

CULTURE IS LARGELY INVISIBLE

What we see of culture is expressed in living artifacts, which include communicated messages such as that of Mr. Chan concerning the food. But they also include human activities such as language, customs, and dress, as well as physical artifacts such as architecture, art, and decoration.

Because much of culture is hidden, these obvious and visible elements of culture may be likened to the tip of an iceberg.[8] Icebergs have as much as 90 percent of their mass below the surface of the water, leaving only a small percentage visible. The important part of the iceberg that is culture is not the obvious physical symbols that are above the surface but the deep underlying values and assumptions that they express. So understanding cultures involves a lot more than just understanding immediate surface behavior such as bows, handshakes, invitations, ceremonies, and body language. The invisible elements of culture—the underlying values, social structures, and ways of thinking—are the most important.

CULTURE MAY BE "TIGHT" OR "LOOSE"

Cultures differ from each other not just in their details but also in their pervasiveness.[9] Some societies are characterized by virtually 100 percent agreement as to the form of correct behavior; other societies may have greater diversity and tolerance of difference. "Tight" cultures have uniformity and agreement and are often based on homogeneous populations or the dominance of particular religious beliefs. Japan is a good example. Countries such as Canada with diverse populations have relatively "loose" cultures, which in some cases are made even looser by the encouragement of freedom of thought and action.

National and Global Culture

As we have mentioned, nation and culture are not identical. Many ethnic cultures, organization cultures, minority cultures, and subcultures may influence different people within the same country. For example, the indigenous peoples of North America have cultural characteristics very different from those of the majority of Canadians and Americans, and both the United States and Canada have many distinctive cultural groupings within their populations. The main focus of this book, however, is on national culture.

Nations are often formed because of cultural similarities among different population groups, and over time they reinforce their adherence to a national culture by means of shared institutions, legal and educational systems, and, of course, nowadays, the mass media. National cultures are particularly important in international business because of the concept of national sovereignty and the need to conduct business affairs within a nation's legal and political frameworks.

Another issue relating to national culture concerns the apparent growth of "global culture." Some people argue that as travel, business, and the media become more international, all countries converge toward a single culture, ironing out all the special differences that make each national culture unique. Because of the economic dominance of Western countries, particularly the United States and the larger European democracies, some people think that these countries' cultural forms will gradually submerge other cultures around the world. Thus, the international proliferation of organizations such as McDonald's and Starbucks is often welcomed as a sign of economic success, while also being criticized as an intrusion of American culture.

If the convergence theory were correct, it might be a reason to downplay the notion of cultural intelligence. If this were the case, it could be best to work with people from all nations to help them to get away from their own cultural habits and instead to understand and practice values and customs that are becoming standard around the world.

We think that this is a bad strategy for several reasons:

1. While some evidence supports the convergence theory, other evidence opposes it.[10] Many cultures may be becom-

ing "modern," but they are doing so in different ways. Cultures tend to accept some aspects of other societies and reject others. In Hong Kong, for example, people have retained their traditional Chinese respect for authority while rejecting its fatalism and have adopted modern competitiveness but rejected modern attitudes toward sexual freedom. Across the world, probably the only real convergence that is taking place is in surface matters such as basic business structures and consumer preferences, rather than in fundamental ways of thinking and behaving.

2. A society may also appear to accept change, but in fact the change is often recontextualized to fit preexisting cultural patterns.[11] For example, even though a McDonald's restaurant may look very much the same in any part of the world, the experience of visiting a McDonald's is very different for Japanese or Chinese or French or U.S. people. That is, people from many Western countries see McDonald's as the place one goes to for fast food, but many Chinese people visit McDonald's as a means of having an "American experience."

3. Even if convergence is taking place, the pace of change is very slow. The evolution of culture in any society is not easily predicted.[12] Traditional cultural patterns tend to be deeply embedded. Those who intend to sit back and wait for the rest of the world to catch up with the West in terms of culture will have to wait for a very long time.

4. Societies worldwide are recognizing the value of diversity in human affairs. Just as biodiversity has a value in allowing ecosystems to deal with major change, so too does cultural diversity offer us a wider range of viewpoints and ways of doing things. Many societies nowadays go out of their way to ensure that cultures under threat are protected from submergence by majority cultures.

Key Cultural Values

In chapter 1, we rejected the laundry-list approach to understanding cultures—learning everything one needs to know about every culture one is likely to deal with—on the basis that cultures are so diverse and so complex that the task is impossible.

Nevertheless, we can "unpackage" cultures by describing their essential features to aid understanding. It is a bit like the language we use to describe people. Sally may be a unique individual with specific qualities and quirks of character that would take a long time to describe. But if we say Sally is intelligent, extroverted, emotionally stable, and unassertive, we have in a few words conveyed a lot of information that might differentiate Sally from other people.

Just as we can summarize people's individual characteristics, we can summarize the characteristics of a culture. An important way to describe both the similarities and differences among cultures is by their underlying values. These cultural values are fundamental shared beliefs about how things should be or how one should behave.

Consider the case below.

HOW ARE YOUR JOB INTERVIEWS GOING?

Barry and Miguel, students approaching graduation at the University of Nevada, are close friends—roommates from their freshman days and keen rivals on the racquetball court. On graduation, each seeks a position in a major company, Barry hopefully on the West Coast of the United States and Miguel in his native Mexico. But their strategies for finding work are quite different.

All the time he has been at university, Barry has focused on developing himself as a unique individual, consciously improving his skills—particularly communication skills—his initiative, his personal goals, and his own identity. He has been powerfully influenced by books that tell him: "You are unique, you are a brand, develop yourself as a product and market yourself and what you bring, to get the highest price and best prospects you can for your services." At corporate interviews, Barry aims to shine. He does not expect to have any particular loyalty to the company that hires him. In a dog-eat-dog world, Barry will, at each stage, move to the best deal he can get: if his initial company continues to offer the best deal, then he will be loyal.

Miguel attends no corporate interviews, not even with companies that he knows have big operations in his native Mexico. When people ask him and Barry, "How are your interviews going?" Barry can answer, but he can't. It is not for him to fix up interviews; it is for his family, particularly his father and his uncles, who own their own small business in Mexico City and have lots of business contacts they will use to secure him openings after graduation. Miguel knows that for him to arrange interviews on his own without his family's blessing would be to commit an unforgivable offense against his parents and the wider family that has always looked after him. He is confident that after he returns to Mexico, he will have interviews, opportunities, and potential jobs, almost certainly arranged through other family members and friends. He knows that he will be expected to take family advice on which opportunities to take, and that long-term loyalty both to the family and to his new employers will be expected. He *wants* to give that loyalty: it's the way things should be.

One night, Barry and Miguel discuss their rapidly approaching careers after a racquetball game. They have difficulty in understanding each other. "How can you let yourself be so dependent on others?" says Barry. "Some people would see it as nepotistic and corrupt." "How can you live your life as a man apart?" says Miguel. "Don't you care about the people who help you? Some people would see you as selfish and ungrateful."

The explanation for the cross-cultural misunderstanding in the case of Barry and Miguel is based on an important dimension of variation between cultures. Latin Americans have a much more group-oriented culture than Americans. Many activities, ranging from the kind of job seeking referred to above to methods of decision making, are based on groups— extended families, organization departments, volunteer groups. This results because of differentiating factors called *individualism* and *collectivism*.

- In *individualist* cultures people are most concerned about the consequences of action for themselves, not others. They prefer activities conducted on one's own or in relatively private interactions with friends. Decisions are made by the individual according to his or her own judgment as to what is appropriate and on the individual rewards that will accrue.

- In *collectivist* cultures, people primarily view themselves as members of groups and collectives rather than as autonomous individuals. They are concerned about the effects of actions on these groups and the approval of other people in their groups. Their activities are more likely to be undertaken in groups on a more public basis. Decisions are made on a consensual or consultative basis, and the effects of the decision on everyone in the social group are taken into account.

Individualism and collectivism are not either/or. They provide dimensions along which different cultures can be understood. Of all measures of cultural variation, individualism and collectivism are the most useful and powerful.[13] However, it is important not to simplify these dimensions by, for example, equating individualism with selfishness or introversion, or collectivism with socialism. Both individualists and collectivists have relationships and groups, but the type of relationship is different: collectivists actually tend to have fewer groups with which they identify, but these are wide, diverse groups such as tribes or extended families, and the bonds of loyalty are strong. Individualists often identify with many different groups, but the bonds are superficial.

Individualism–collectivism potentially provides a basis for

describing national culture in terms of its position on the dimension between them, and for comparing any two national cultures on the same basis. When other dimensions or aspects of culture are added to the picture, somewhat more detailed assessments and comparisons can be made.

HOFSTEDE'S STUDY

For example, in Geert Hofstede's well-known survey of over 100,000 employees of a large multinational corporation spread across fifty countries, each country, on the basis of its employees' responses, was assigned an individualism score between 1 and 100.[14] The most individualist countries on this measure were Australia, Belgium, Canada, Great Britain, Israel, Italy, New Zealand, South Korea, and the United States, all of which had scores of over 75. Collectivist countries that scored less than 20 included Chile, Colombia, Costa Rica, El Salvador, Guatemala, Indonesia, Pakistan, Panama, Peru, Taiwan, and Venezuela. The countries with high scores were all North American, European, or former colonies of the United Kingdom. The lower scores were found in countries in South America and East Asia. Among countries that came out around the average for individualism-collectivism were Argentina, India, Japan, and Spain.

INDIVIDUALISM AND COLLECTIVISM

As we have shown, individualism is most common in developed Western countries. A strong relationship exists between a country's individualism and its wealth (gross national product, or GNP).[15] The recent political fashion of free markets and the encouragement of entrepreneurship plays to individualism, and developed countries have seen a marked international trend in this direction, leading, for example, to a general decline in individuals' loyalty to their employing organizations. Try the exercise in the appendix to see the extent to which you think of yourself in individualist or collectivist terms.

Individualism and collectivism, while perhaps the most important dimensions of cultural variation, are not the only dimensions that researchers have been able to identify. For example, Israeli psychologist Shalom Schwartz and his colleagues did a more recent and more sophisticated mapping of cultures according to their value orientations.[16] They identified three universal requirements that every culture has of itself: the need to specify how individuals should relate to the wider society, the need for society to preserve itself, and the need to define how society should relate to the natural world. Schwartz's idea was that while all societies have to address these requirements, they do so in different ways. In each society this leads to a shared set of fundamental beliefs about how things should be or how one should behave. By examining fifty-seven national cultures, Schwartz and colleagues derived seven fundamental value dimensions:

- Egalitarianism—recognition of people as moral equals
- Harmony—fitting in harmoniously with the environment
- Embeddedness—people as part of a collective
- Hierarchy—unequal distribution of power
- Mastery—exploitation of the natural or social environment
- Affective autonomy—pursuit of positive experiences
- Intellectual autonomy—independent pursuit of one's own ideas

Figure 2.2 shows the relative positions of countries along the seven dimensions.

It is impossible to represent perfectly the relative position of countries on seven dimensions in the two-dimensional space of the printed page. However, by using a technique called a coplot, Schwartz and his colleagues were able to present the relationships quite accurately. The position of each country along

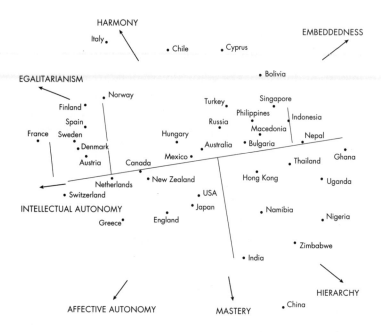

FIGURE 2.2.   Co-plot of value dimensions across national cultures
Source: Adapted from Sagiv & Schwartz (2000)

the vector of each cultural dimension indicates how similar or different each country is on that dimension. For example, Canada and New Zealand are very similar on all seven dimensions. However, the United States, which is similar to these two countries on other dimensions, ranks higher on the mastery dimension (more like Japan). By examining the position of your own country and that of others on this map, or by reading Schwartz's books and papers—or indeed Hofstede's—you can increase your knowledge about the areas of potential cultural harmony or conflict with members of another culture.

THE GLOBE STUDY

Another way of understanding similarities and differences across cultures is to examine which countries cluster together in their positions on various measures of cultural values. Based on a large-scale study of cultural differences in values, researchers who conducted the Global Leadership and Organizational Behaviour Effectiveness (GLOBE) study grouped the sixty-two societies they studied into ten clusters.[17] These clusters, shown in figure 2.3, are based on overall similarity of countries based on nine value orientations:

- *Institutional Collectivism:* The degree to which organizational and societal institutional practices encourage and reward collective distribution of resources and collective action

- *In-Group Collectivism:* The degree to which individuals express pride, loyalty, and cohesiveness in their organizations or families

- *Power Distance:* The degree to which members of a collective expect power to be distributed unequally

- *Uncertainty Avoidance:* The extent to which a society, organization, or group relies on social norms, rules, and procedures to alleviate unpredictability of future events

- *Gender Egalitarianism:* The degree to which a collective minimizes gender inequality

- *Assertiveness:* The degree to which individuals are assertive, confrontational, and aggressive in their relationships with others

- *Humane Orientation:* The degree to which a collective rewards individuals for being fair, altruistic, generous, caring, and kind to others

- *Future Orientation:* The extent to which individuals engage in future-oriented behaviors such as delayed gratification, planning, and investing in the future

- *Performance Orientation:* The degree to which a collective encourages and rewards group members for performance improvement and excellence

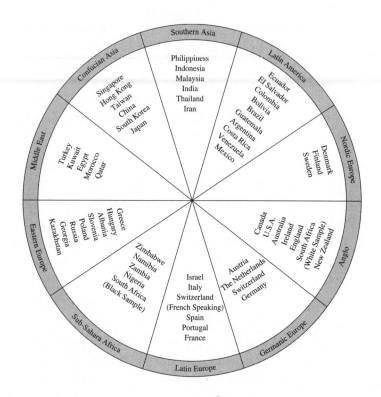

FIGURE 2.3. Country clusters according to GLOBE

As shown in figure 2.3, the clusters of countries reflect such factors as common language, common religion, common climate, geographic proximity, common economic system, and shared political boundaries—all of which can be shown to contribute to national cultural variation.[18] This typology underscores the historical basis of cultural variation. For example, the composition of the Anglo cluster indicates that as a result of migration this culture was diffused from England to Ireland, the United States, Canada, South Africa, Australia, and New Zealand, and its position relative to other clusters indicates its own roots in Saxony (Germany) and Jutland (northern Denmark). Likewise the Confucian Asian cultural cluster reflects the strong historical influence of China and Confucian ideology. Even Japan with its physical isolation shared significant cultural interactions with China over time. As with the mapping of the Schwartz value orientations, by referring to the GLOBE cultural clusters, you can get a first approximation of the extent to which you might share cultural values with people from other societies.

Effects of Culture: The "In-Group" and the "Out-Group"

An important aspect of culture is the way we use it to define ourselves. If we state that we are "American," "Thai," "Muslim," or that we "work for IBM," our assertion places us inside a boundary that excludes a lot of other people. It differentiates us. It sets up expectations—intentional or unintentional—as to the kinds of attitudes and behavior that others can expect from us.

This tendency is important in terms of bias—typically bias is in favor of our own group or culture (the "in-group"), and against others (the "out-group") external to our own. Therefore, we typically discriminate in our own group's favor.

Most importantly, we tend to identify everything about the in-group as being normal (i.e., the way things ought to be done). Consequently, whenever we encounter people doing things a different way, we tend to see their action as not just different but as deviant, even as wrong. We are particularly likely to do this when operating on our own turf, yet even when we are overseas we tend to take our own common experiences at home as the norm for how others ought to behave.

For example, although the United States and Mexico are geographically close to each other, the GLOBE clusters suggest that they are separated by a significant cultural distance. The GLOBE value scores for the two countries and the average for the entire worldwide sample (on a scale of 1 to 7) are as follows:[19]

GLOBE DIMENSION	UNITED STATES	MEXICO	WORLD AVERAGE
Assertiveness	4.36	3.67	3.82
Institutional Collectivism	4.20	4.77	4.73
In-Group Collectivism	5.79	5.78	5.66
Future Orientation	5.35	5.74	5.49
Gender Egalitarianism	5.03	4.57	4.51
Humane Orientation	5.51	5.10	5.42
Performance Orientation	6.14	6.00	5.94
Power Distance	2.88	2.75	2.75
Uncertainty Avoidance	3.99	5.18	4.62

The table shows that the United States has a very high level of assertiveness, performance orientation, and gender egalitarianism as compared to the world average and to Mexico. Mexico, on the other hand, has very high uncertainty avoidance compared to the world average and the United States. It is easy to see how it might be difficult for individuals from one country to know how to behave socially in another country or to understand the process of making decisions in still another when those countries are from different groups.

As in the case of Barry and Miguel presented previously in the chapter, consider how an American and a Mexican with no prior cross-cultural experience might perceive each other from the standpoint of their own cultures. Despite some very different scores in both countries, individuals from each are likely to judge the other as though his or her own country represents the norm. Each will take "the way we do things at home" as a starting point. The American may find irritating Mexicans' emphasis on social activity, the slowness of their consultative decision making, their comfort with status differences between men and women, and their discomfort with any sort of ambiguity or with taking decisive action on their own initiative. For their part, the Mexican might see Americans as being self-centered, aggressive, and single-mindedly focused on performance.

The first step to cultural flexibility is to *understand your own culture* and how it affects your interpretation of the behavior of others. This is an important part—though far from the only part—of the cultural makeup and stereotyping that you most likely bring to each new cross-cultural situation you face. We have already suggested that you locate your own culture in terms of the Schwartz map or the GLOBE clusters. Think about your culture again in terms of all its special features and idiosyncrasies. Try to look at it through the eyes of people from contrasting cultures.

Summary

This chapter describes how knowledge of what culture is and how it varies and affects behavior is the first stage of developing cultural intelligence. Culture is not a random assortment of customs and behaviors. It is the values, attitudes, and assumptions about behavior that are shared by people in specific groups. It is systematic and organized and has developed over time as a result of societies learning to deal with their common problems. Cultures can be defined according to their values—the fundamental beliefs that people within the culture share about how things should be and how one should behave. Culture is shared; it is passed on from one generation to the next. While it has a profound influence on behavior, the most important aspects of culture are invisible. A key feature of culture is that it categorizes others and us into in-groups and out-groups. This categorization of people into "them and us" underlies much cross-cultural behavior. There are several important dimensions along which cultures can be defined, the most important being individualism and collectivism. By understanding our own culture we can then make initial comparisons with others to understand areas of possible agreement or disagreement. The knowledge gained in this way is a necessary first step to becoming culturally intelligent. In subsequent chapters we link this knowledge with the important elements of mindfulness and cross-cultural skills.

CHAPTER 3

Mindfulness and Cross-Cultural Skills

UNDERSTANDING SHANICE

Katherine Davis has had a good start in life. From a privileged New York family, the daughter of a renowned surgeon, Katherine attended Harvard Medical School and at the age of twenty-five is qualified as a medical doctor. Katherine is not sure, however, which of the specialist medical options she wishes to pursue, and for her first full-time job, to broaden her experience and to try working for a few months at least in what she thinks of as the "concrete jungle" of inner-city life, she has chosen a humble position in a run-down clinic in a poor area of Washington, DC.

Katherine's experience with her very first patient is a shattering one. On her first morning on duty, she encounters Shanice Jackson, who blows into her office, flourishes some empty medicine bottles, and demands refills for her asthma medication. Which would be fine, if it weren't for the fact that Shanice is only twelve years old and is on her own, unaccompanied by any adult. The problem is not financial—everything is covered by Medicaid—but Katherine is a little shocked. So she gets the impatient Shanice—who apparently had a good relationship with Katherine's predecessor and calls in regularly to replenish her medications—to sit down and wait while she checks Shanice's case notes. Shanice would rather get what she wants and leave, but Katherine makes it clear that that won't happen until she knows a bit more.

The notes reveal that Shanice has chronic asthma and major allergies that frequently cause her to wheeze and cough through the night. Her brother, who shares the bedroom, often complains about it. Her school attendance is poor, with many days missed for reasons that might be medical but might not. She apparently lives with her grandmother, who is referred to in the notes as "Grandma Jones." She attends the clinic frequently to replenish her supply of drugs to control her asthma and provide quick relief in the event of an attack. Neither Grandma Jones nor any other adult has accompanied her to the clinic since her first visit two years ago, and all attempts by the busy clinic to contact her grandmother have failed. It's clear that Shanice, although she is only a child, has taken responsibility for her own medical care. Although she brings along empty bottles, it's not possible to determine whether she has taken her medicine appropriately or whether the other instructions the clinic have given her about how to take day-to-day precautions to prevent asthma attacks are being followed. From what Shanice says, Grandma Jones, despite being Shanice's legal guardian, hasn't the slightest interest in her illness.

Katherine is bewildered. What is going on here? Where are Shanice's parents? Why did the *grandmother* take Shanice to the clinic in the first place, and why is she now ignoring her obvious responsibility? Doesn't she care? Why does a twelve-year-old have to manage her own medical care? The more Katherine thinks about it, the madder she gets.

This case deals with subcultures—cultures within cultures, in this case white upper-middle-class America versus black urban-poor America—rather than cultures. The problem for Katherine is that she knows only half the story and is judging it from her own cultural background where the expectation—if no longer the norm—is two middle-class parents, no additional dependents, enough money to go around, available transport and time, good mental health in all parties, an attitude of cocooning children from potential harm, and a rational belief in modern medical science.

Maybe Shanice's parents are dead, or possibly they have long ago absolved themselves of any responsibility for her. In African American families grandparents are often caregivers. Maybe Grandma Jones has to work full-time as well as meeting her family responsibilities, just in order to feed them. Maybe she can't get to the clinic because it's open at the wrong times and she doesn't have a car. Maybe she has stresses in her life that the clinic staff can hardly imagine. Maybe she or Shanice's mother or Shanice's brother suffers from depression or other mental illness. Maybe Grandma Jones is religious or superstitious or has her own negative memories of the health care system or has her own ideas about how to cure asthma. Maybe the family has conflicts over what is best.

Katherine is judging the case from a different set of cultural standards. She is in what we would term "cultural cruise control," with her own values and attitudes about how life should be lived dominating her judgment of Grandma Jones, a woman she has never met.

You can't judge people by projecting your own norms for behavior onto them. You have to look at the context such as their economic situations, the resources available to them, and most of all the culture or subculture that their behavior is coming out of.

This example shows that cultural differences are not just abstractions. They become part and parcel of the behavior of people from all cultures. In our day-to-day behavior we unconsciously act according to cultural norms—patterns of behavior specific to a particular culture.

In this chapter we look at how our cultural norms help us, but also hinder us in our dealings with others, particularly culturally different others, by providing a "cultural cruise control" that we rely on to guide our actions. We show how it is often necessary to break out of our cultural cruise control by practicing *mindfulness,* a kind of thoughtful attention to cues provided by other people, situations, and cultures, and as a result to develop new cross-cultural *skills*. The combination of knowledge (see chapter 2), mindfulness, and cross-cultural skills is the basis of cultural intelligence.

Cultural Cruise Control

A good way of thinking about the patterns of behavior described above is through the use of the term "script."[1] In the theater, a script tells the actor what he or she is supposed to say and sometimes gives guidance about how it should be said. In cultural rituals such as initiation ceremonies the script is often precise. But other scripts allow more scope for individual interpretation (see discussion of "tight" versus "loose" cultures in chapter 2). There are scripts for Americans and scripts for Chinese, for instance, but they have some allowance for individual variation. For example, it may be possible within the workplace script of an American to be playfully disrespectful to a superior, but it would never be so for a Chinese.

Norms and scripts help us by telling us what to do. They prescribe patterns of behavior that feel comfortable for us because we observe them being practiced by members of the in-group to which we belong or aspire to belong. The real problems occur when the norms and scripts of one culture clash with those of another (as in the Shanice case, for example) because, in order to interact, we must not only act out our own scripts, but also observe and make sense of others' actions based on *their* scripts. To do this we have to break out of our scripted behavior and switch off our cultural cruise control.

Cultural cruise control means running your life on the basis of your built-in cultural assumptions. We call it cruise control because people let it happen automatically, without thinking about it. But it can be damaging because of the way it causes them to ignore other cultural signals.

In the case that opened this chapter, Katherine Davis is

operating on cultural cruise control with regard to middle-class conventions about health care. She is unable to move outside the standard assumptions that prescribe behavior in her culture. If she were to exercise the principles we describe in this chapter for getting out of cultural cruise-control mode, she would gain much greater insight and might be able to help Shanice more. For example, Katherine perhaps needs to talk to colleagues in the clinic about the nature of the urban culture she has become involved with. She needs to walk around the neighborhood to get some idea of how people there live. She should get Shanice to talk about her situation and should listen to what she says. She should tell herself, "I'm not at Harvard now." All these will help her to turn off cultural cruise control and get a better sense of the new culture she has found herself involved with.

Mindlessness

If you want to develop cultural intelligence, you need to be able to suspend cultural cruise control and develop an alternative state of being called mindfulness.[2] A good starting point to understanding mindfulness is to examine its alternative—mindlessness—in the everyday activity of driving an automobile.

Driving is a good example of mindlessness. Living is complex, but through superior learning abilities we humans have learned to simplify it by developing sequences of complex actions that we perform competently without paying conscious attention. Driving is one such routine. When driving, we can almost unconsciously steer, avoid obstacles, operate direction indicators, and brake when appropriate. While we drive we can simultaneously listen to the news on the radio, reflect on the day's work, plan the evening meal, or have a conversation with a passenger. When we follow familiar routes, we can even forget about navigating the car. Have you ever had the experience of arriving at your workplace or your home in your car after following a familiar route and noting with surprise, "I'm here! How did I get here? I guess I was thinking about something else!"?

Mindlessness is not necessarily negative—in driving it simply means we drive without having our minds fully engaged on the job. If we can do so safely, why not? Mindlessness has its advantages. It makes it possible for us to do more than one thing at a time. It enables us to ignore much of what goes on around us or to fit it automatically into an existing framework. It enables us to "get on with our lives."

However, the benefits of mindlessness are short-term and may be illusory. Mindlessness encourages us to rely on routine and prevents us from being flexible in changing circumstances. For example, businesspeople who have been successful in the past mindlessly continue with the same approaches and techniques that brought them success and fail to notice that circumstances have changed. International managers from developed countries mindlessly assume that their role is to enlighten their counterparts in transition economies on "correct" actions in a market economy, even though such actions may be totally inappropriate for the different situation. Tourists traveling abroad mindlessly search menus in vain for their "back home" favorite dishes. These are all examples of trying to let cruise control do the work in changing conditions for which it was not designed.

Sources of Cultural Scripts

From an early age, we carry elements of our culture around with us. Much learning is imitative. As children, we imitate the attitudes and behavior of our parents and other role models.[3] We become aware of ideas and ways of acting that are considered normal within the confines of our own culture. There are also the deliberate practices of socialization—learning programs at home, in school, in peer groups, and so forth—where we learn new rules of action, often derived from the culture or subculture.

For most of us, cultural cruise control makes our own culture the center of our mental universe and causes us to regard all others as deviant. Scripts from other cultures are not considered, and, if practiced by others, are likely to be unnoticed, ignored, or misunderstood. Even if what we learn is simply unease in the presence of those from other cultures, or a feeling that they are odd, this discomfort is likely to be built into our cruise control.

Cultural cruise control tends to work just fine as long as we are with people with whom we share underlying cultural assumptions—most likely people from the same background and social class, as well as culture. The cultural differences we indicated in chapter 2 build in powerful assumptions too, almost like little voices urging others to *Be Like Me!* As long as others share the same cultural grounding, we can take culture for granted and focus on other matters. But when we are interacting with people whose cultural background is different, errors and misunderstandings quickly emerge, and our relationships are undermined.

We have all been in situations where someone has, to use an expression beloved by the English, "dropped a clanger" (that is, unwittingly said or done something offensive to the religion, ethnicity, background, or beliefs of someone else present). An example is putting out your hand to shake the hand of an orthodox Jew, not realizing that this familiarity is prohibited by his customs. Most clangers are caused by one person's continuing to make the assumptions of his or own culture without noticing that the other person has his or her own background and customs and should be treated differently.

How Culture Affects Behavior[4]

Cultural programming also acts as a mental template against which new information from "out there"—the environment— is interpreted. We are not cameras: we do not take in neutral information from out there and reproduce it exactly on the film of our minds. We perceive information with cultural and other cues embedded in it and interpret it in light of our own preconceived frameworks. In the process, differences and distortions occur.

SELECTIVE PERCEPTION

At any given time, we can attend to only a fraction of the myriad of ever-changing stimuli the world presents us. When in cruise-control mode, we rely on our mental programming and screen out all that is not immediately and directly relevant. For example, in an emergency situation when driving, we perceive information relevant to the emergency—the road, traffic, the sound of the car engine—and do not notice the expressions on the faces of passersby, the color of the upholstery in the car, or the music still playing on the car radio. Cultural conditioning teaches us what to perceive and what to ignore: people from different cultures can be presented with exactly the same situation and perceive it differently.

Suppose you are eating with someone at a restaurant, and he or she is talking about a business deal. If you are interested in business, you will pay close attention to the words. But if you are, for example, a fashion expert or a chef, you may be more interested in what your companion is wearing or eating, and if you are romantically interested you may attend to what they look, sound, and smell like. If you are from a collectivist society, you may look for information about the person's relationship with family or group, and if you are from an individualist society, for evidence of the person's personal attainments. Your culture is one of the key factors that focuses your attention.

SOCIAL CATEGORIZATION

Another key mental process that helps us deal with all the information presented to us is called categorization. This process involves sorting other people (and ourselves) into different categories just as postal workers sort mail into pigeonholes. Each hole might be labeled with the last few digits of a postal code. As letters are sorted, the postal worker does not read the name or address on the letter but glances only at the postal code in order to put the letter in the proper bin. In this way the amount of information that must be dealt with by the sorter is greatly reduced. In order to be similarly efficient, we categorize people based on limited information.

Often we categorize others on the basis of appearance; in other cases we must attend to additional cues. Speech— language, accent, vocabulary, content—is an important source of cues. We tend to make in-group and out-group categorizations (see chapter 2); that is, we classify people according to whether they belong, or do not belong, to groups of which we ourselves are members.

Other key indicators enable us to sort people into categories. Examples are:

- race and gender
- the extent to which a person stands out as different from others (for example, Europeans are obvious in rural Japan)
- being "typical" of a particular group
- a history of conflict with a group, leading to categorization as "not in our group"

Once we form a category, we perceive its members to be similar to each other. In contrast, we continue to see differences between members of our own group. For example, an Asian person may be broadly aware of a category of "European," whereas a European may see many different categories within "European"—for example, Anglo Saxon, Celtic, Mediterranean, Scandinavian, and Slav, not to mention different national and regional categories.

STEREOTYPING

Categorizing people influences our attitudes about and expectations of them.[5] We tend to perceive everyone in the group as having particular characteristics and similar behaviors. We may expect Americans to be noisy, Irish gregarious, and Japanese polite. These stereotypes need not be negative but often are. When stereotypes contain negative attitudes and expectations, they often lead to negative behavior or prejudice. Perhaps the most noxious prejudice toward others who are "not like me" is racism, in part because it is so easy to categorize others based on race.[6] Stereotypes of other nationalities may be intense, particularly when the group in question is prominent in one's experience. Much political conflict—for instance, Arab-Israeli, Indian-Pakistani, Serbian-Kosovar, Irish Catholic-Irish Protestant—creates and is supported by intense negative stereotypes of out-groups. Stereotypes may be based on limited information or on the views of influential others. People can hold intense stereotypes of another culture without ever having met anyone from that culture. Furthermore, stereotypes perpetuate themselves, because through selective perception (see above), we tend to notice events and behavior that confirm our stereotypes and fail to notice information that disconfirms them.

ATTRIBUTION

In attribution we move beyond simple observation and interpretation of others to make inferences about *why* people might behave as they do. Particularly important is the distinction between internal attributions, in which behavior is attributed to factors associated with the person (for example, "she punished her son because she is an aggressive person") and external attributions, in which we believe behavior is caused by external circumstance ("she punished her son because he misbehaved").

When categorization and stereotypic expectations are combined with attribution, we get some interesting effects. For example, "she punished her son because she is Serbian, and Serbians are well known to be cruel and aggressive people."

A common error is to attribute the behavior of members

of an out-group to the same causes that would likely be true if members of our own in-group behaved the same way, as shown in the case below.

THE BOYFRIEND WHO WASN'T

A young American[7] man devoted a lot of attention to a Japanese woman visiting his community, including extreme courtesy—taking her arm to cross the street, and so on. The young woman later told her friends excitedly that she now had an American boyfriend. In fact, the American, who was from the Deep South of the United States where many families pride themselves on effusive courtesy, was not interested in the Japanese girl as a prospective girlfriend. He had merely tried to be polite, in a manner that came naturally to him in his own in-group. Unfortunately, the same type of behavior practiced by a member of the Japanese woman's in-group would definitely have been evidence of a romantic interest.[8]

In this case, cultural cruise control affected both parties. The American man continued to act automatically in the script of his own culture, without noticing the impression his behavior was making on his companion. The Japanese woman continued to observe automatically through the lens of her own culture and made no allowances for the difference in background. Without either one meaning to, the two colluded to create a major misunderstanding. What was needed was for one or both to *switch off their cultural cruise control* and adopt a state of mindfulness in which they both become aware of the cultural significance of their own and the other's behavior.

Switching Off Cultural Cruise Control

A pilot whose airplane is set in cruise control—automatic pilot—knows that he or she can rely on the expert programming built into the automatic system to keep the plane flying straight and level and on the correct course, as long as conditions stay normal. But once in a while a change in conditions—a sudden weather hazard, a mechanical failure, or even the need to land the plane—will trigger warning signs. The pilot will snap out of mindlessness, switch off the automatic pilot, and devote all of his or her attention and skill to the problem.

If a person from the United States tries to drive a car in Japan or the United Kingdom, where the traffic travels on the left side of the road rather than the right and the driving controls are on the right side of the car not the left, he or she will initially have to abandon some of the built-in rules and habits used when driving in the United States. In novel cross-cultural situations, it is imperative that we consciously switch off our cultural cruise control. However, doing so is just the first step. Suspending cultural mindlessness means that you are attending to cultural issues. It does not follow that you are attending to them in a productive way. To get maximum benefit requires a new set of active practices, which we call mindfulness.

Mindfulness

Mindfulness is the opposite of mindlessness. Mindfulness is such a common idea that most of us do not appreciate how powerful it can be. It is basically *paying attention* to context. It means discarding our rigid mental programming. It does not mean abandoning who we are but rather using attention to become aware of differences and to think differently. It includes the recognition that despite cultural differences there will also be many similarities between us and people from other groups, and that the cultural differences that do exist do not matter all the time.

In cross-cultural interactions, mindfulness means simultaneously paying attention to the external situation, monitoring our own thoughts and feelings, and regulating the knowledge and skills we use.

MINDFUL ATTENTION

Mindful attention means using all of the senses in perceiving situations (for example hearing the words that the other person speaks but also noting the expression on his or her face), viewing the situation with an open mind, and attending to the context to help interpret what is happening.

MINDFUL MONITORING

Mindful monitoring means being aware of our own assumptions, ideas, and emotions, as well as noticing what is apparent about the other people and tuning in to their assumptions, words, and behavior. It also means putting ourselves in other people's shoes as a means of understanding the situation and their feelings toward it, from the perspective of their cultural background rather than ours.

MINDFUL REGULATION

Mindful regulation means creating new mental maps of other people's personalities and cultural backgrounds to assist in responding appropriately to them, creating new categories and recategorizing others into a more sophisticated system, seeking out fresh information to confirm or disconfirm the mental maps, choosing not to respond automatically, and editing responses to be consistent with our goals.

For example:

Mindlessness: "After I finished the job, she started criticizing me. She is always criticizing me. She is Asian and doesn't understand how we do things here. So I stopped listening to her. She went on and on, and eventually I just walked out."

Mindfulness: "After I finished the job, she started criticizing the way I had done it. I listened to what she had to say; maybe she would have some good points to make. I paid attention to the tone of her voice and the way she looked: she didn't really seem angry, just concerned. I was aware that I hadn't done that sort of work before, that she was more experienced. I knew she would have to explain the problem to her boss, and I wondered how that would feel for her. She is Asian, and I knew she would not want to lose face. But she is so knowledgeable; I knew I could learn from her. I also knew she didn't like to be interrupted, so I waited patiently till she was finished. Then I apologized for my mistakes, thanked her for her feedback, and asked if she could monitor me while I did the job again."

Mindfulness is a mediating step that helps us to link knowledge to skillful practice. It gives us readiness to interact with people who are different. It gives us the background to communicate comfortably and accurately in ways that honor the backgrounds and identities of both parties. And it focuses our mental abilities on the cross-cultural aspects of the situation.

Being mindful takes a lot of effort, especially at first. But over time being mindful can become a natural and normal way of being. We don't have to be mindful all the time. But mindfulness helps us to be in control and leads to greater freedom of thought and action.

Cross-Cultural Skills

Knowledge and mindfulness are key elements in cultural intelligence, but in themselves they are not enough. In practice, cultural intelligence is seen in and judged by *skilled behavior*. Cultural intelligence is not just a mind game—you have to be able to *perform*.

For example, in the case with which we started this chapter, it is insufficient for Dr. Katherine Davis to understand Shanice's and Grandma Jones's cultural background and to be able to pay mindful attention to them. She also needs to be able to interact with them in a suitable way so that they feel relaxed, confident, and able to work with her to reach a good conclusion.

The third and last element of cultural intelligence is *cross-cultural skills*. Behavioral scientists have long been aware that the concept of skill can be applied to social behavior. In business, for example, the most commonly perceived causes of problems are not technical or administrative deficiencies but problems such as communication failures, misunderstandings in negotiations, personality conflicts, poor leadership style, and bad teamwork—in other words, inadequacies in the ways that people interact with each other.

Nowadays, many organizations regard social skills or interpersonal skills as key qualifications for new employees. Upward of 70 percent of most managers' time, in most cultures, is typically spent in interaction with others—superiors, subordinates, peers, clients, and others—in face-to-face conversations, meetings, telephone calls, and informal social settings.[9] Skilled interpersonal performance is vital, and many companies offer skills training as part of their employee development programs. Marital relationships similarly benefit from good interpersonal skills.

Most of us at one time or another have admired the social performance of colleagues and others who are virtuosi in the art of interpersonal communication and relationship building. Each of us also, to a greater or lesser degree, has our own set of skilled social behaviors, and these are closely related to the expectations and scripts of our own culture. Some of the social skills we develop in our own cultures may contain elements—such as willingness to initiate a conversation, interest in other people, and listening skills—that may assist us in other cultural settings. However, operating in other cultures also creates a new frontier for our social interactions, probably requiring the development of new social performance.

Acquiring the skills of cultural intelligence is not about becoming more skilled in a particular behavior or set of behaviors but about building general skills that extend the range, or *repertoire,* of skilled behaviors and knowing when to use each one. Cultural difference extends the range of possibilities that we may face.[10] Skilled routines we have mastered to a high level of performance in one culture may be counterproductive in another, to the extent that we have to "unlearn" them in the new situation. Here is a case in point.

FRENCH DRESSING

Philippe LeBeau was a stereotypically dark, handsome Frenchman. He was known particularly as a ladies' man who knew how to be charming to women and help them to feel good about themselves. This was particularly important in the Paris media company where Philippe worked as a manager, because the majority of employees were women.

Philippe had noticed that many of the women in the company took pride in dressing fashionably and well. He therefore made a point of complimenting them frequently on their appearance—for example, "Marie, that is such a chic outfit! You look as beautiful today as I have ever seen you." This kind of comment almost always gained him a smile, a blush, a thank you, and more importantly, he felt, increased cooperation from the woman to whom he had paid the compliment.

One day it was announced that Philippe's company had been taken over by a major international conglomerate based in the United States. When the dust of the merger had settled, Philippe was delighted to find he was to be transferred for a two-year assignment to the company headquarters in New Jersey. He was given a briefing on the United States and its different social norms and was advised, for example, that touching other people, particularly those of the opposite sex, was much less acceptable there than in France. He therefore resolved to be careful about his French habit of showing positive feelings to his French colleagues by occasionally taking their hands in his, kissing them on the cheek, and the like.

In New Jersey, his new secretary, Anita Courtenay, turned out to be a highly effective person as well as a strikingly beautiful one, who, like many of his French colleagues, dressed extremely well. Philippe was careful to keep his physical distance from Anita as he had been taught, but he felt that her obvious glamour provided an opportunity to build a good relationship. So in his customary French manner he would greet her every morning with a freshly minted compliment on her appearance. Her initial reaction was surprise. Then she would thank him politely and change the subject. But after a week or so she began to respond by frowning and pursing her lips. Philippe was puzzled. She really was an outstanding secretary as well as a beautiful woman. Did she think his compliments were insincere? And was it his imagination, or was she wearing less chic outfits with each passing day? Was she also using less makeup?

On the third morning of Philippe's second week at work, he arrived at his office to find Anita seated at her desk, apparently wearing no makeup and with an outfit that was neat and tasteful but that did nothing to show off the beauty of its wearer. However, even in such modest attire, Anita looked fresh and lovely, and Philippe said so: "Anita, once more you are looking wonderful. Seeing your beauty makes my heart beat faster, and I know that I will work better today because of it."

She looked at him with astonishment and then slowly got to her feet. "Mr. LeBeau," she said levelly, "I want you to stop making comments on my personal appearance. I am not here as a decoration, I am here as an employee. I take a real pride in what I do, but all you can talk about is the way I look. Can you imagine how that makes me feel? I have tried to discourage you, but it seems you won't take a hint. And if you have any ideas about getting involved with me, you can forget them—I have a boyfriend and I don't want another. So from now on, can you please treat me with a bit more respect and professionalism?"

In this case, Philippe has developed a repertoire of skilled behavior that works well in one cultural situation but breaks down in another. His performance is based on a particular "French" view of the world, on ways of expressing himself most likely developed from childhood, on sheer habit, and on having had the habit consistently rewarded. It will be hard for Philippe LeBeau, socially skilled as he is, to erase the habits that don't work in his new environment and to replace them with new, appropriate forms of social performance. First he will need to gain a better understanding of the norms of male-female interaction in his new culture (knowledge). Then he will have to pay more attention to the behavioral cues provided by Anita and the other women with whom he interacts (mindfulness). Lastly he will need to develop new ways of behaving toward women; he will have to experiment with and refine them.

The development of this new behavior depends on developing a set of general skills. The general skills that research has shown to be related to appropriate behavior in cross-cultural interactions are as follows:[11]

- relational skills
- tolerance for uncertainty
- empathy
- perceptual acuity
- adaptability

The specific behavioral skills that are required by managers operating across cultures span the gamut of interactions and interpersonal relationships in organizations.

Skilled Performance

One way of understanding the skills aspect of cultural intelligence is to think of yourself as a *performer*. The notion of skilled performance has been applied to many different areas of human endeavor. Diana Krall singing a jazz standard or Tiger Woods hitting a perfect drive epitomizes the smooth and apparently effortless production of behaviors that exercise near-perfect control over parts of the physical world. These virtuoso performers have enormous physical and mental talent in their chosen fields, yet each has also spent many years of hard work perfecting her or his art. Woods's performance is built on numerous skills, such as manual dexterity and distance estimation, and Krall's on other skills, such as the ability to hear different musical tones and mastery of voice control. The performance of effective cross-cultural behavior is built on general skills such as those indicated above, and sometimes on skills specific to particular cultural situations.

A key skill element in cultural intelligence is *adaptability*. Whether or not social behavior takes place in a cross-cultural setting, each situation will be unique and will involve interaction with other people who are unique. As skilled social performers, we have to be able instantaneously to adapt our general approach and specific interactions to the particular characteristics of the situation and to the expectations of the other people involved. Effective cross-cultural behavior is not composed of fixed routines but of flexible abilities that can—with the guidance of mindfulness—be modified to meet new or changing conditions. Even within a given culture people vary in the extent to which they conform to underlying cultural norms. The culturally intelligent person's social performance draws on a repertoire of potential behaviors. By mindfully monitoring the environment, he or she is able to select, employ, and modify appropriate routines from this wide resource.

Summary

This chapter describes the ways in which our cultural programming affects our behavior and our interactions with others who are culturally different. Much of the time we base our actions on a cultural cruise control in which our mental programming directs our behavior without much conscious thought. This programming allows us to go about our daily routines without actively thinking about everything we do. However, in cross-cultural interactions this mindless behavior can cause problems. Through selective perception, stereotypic expectations, and inaccurate attributions, we may be led by our cultural programming to misjudge the behavior of others who are culturally different. To counteract the tendency to function on cultural cruise control, this book advocates practicing mindfulness, an active awareness that is a critical link between knowledge about culture and appropriate behavior in cross-cultural situations. The culturally intelligent person also needs to increase his or her repertoire of skilled behaviors, particularly social behaviors, and to be able to deploy these appropriately in different cultural settings. The elements of knowledge, mindfulness, and skills enable the practice of cultural intelligence in skilled performance that is adapted to the particular cultural settings the individual faces.

CHAPTER 4

Making Decisions
across Cultures

WHO DESERVES THE BONUS?

Santoso, an Indonesian, and Alice Hughes, an Australian, have been friends and business partners for five years, working tough road-building projects in Indonesia, where Alice's civil engineering background and Santoso's local knowledge and financial skills have provided an ideal complement to each other. Now, however, they find they have a major disagreement.

What has happened is this. Two years ago, A, a senior manager in the company who is independently wealthy and has high status and good networks in his local community, used his status and connections in the area to secure for the company a major project for the building of a section of new road. As far as Santoso and Alice were concerned, the project was a godsend, because they had been facing an uncertain period with few contracts. Moreover, due to the hard work and skill of a number of staff, the project has been very successful, has come in well under budget, and has made a large profit for the company. Believing as they do in sharing good fortune with those who made it possible, Santoso and Alice have decided to set aside the sum of US$100,000 for distribution to the senior personnel involved. The question they have to decide is, who gets paid a bonus, and how much?

Three staff members immediately stand out. A undoubtedly secured the contract but had little to do with the actual completion of the project. B, who is a very smart engineer, wrote a brilliant plan for the project, but thereafter was distracted by a looming family tragedy. He is from a very poor background, has a large family, and struggles to pay his bills: recently his son has been stricken with a brain tumor, and the family faces a bill for overseas treatment that is simply beyond their means given their current income and other commitments. Finally, as the project manager, C managed the project enthusiastically, leading and motivating his project team extremely well to far exceed the project objectives.

How should one go about distributing $100,000 to reward three such distinctive contributions? Alice suggests to Santoso that each of them should individually write down what he or she thinks of as a fair allocation and that they can then use these starting points to negotiate what is fair. Santoso doesn't like that idea—he would prefer a general discussion of the three candidates first. But eventually he agrees.

Alice thinks hard about the allocation and then writes down:

> A: $10,000
>
> B: $50,000
>
> C: $40,000

When she looks at Santoso's sheet of paper, she is shocked. He has written:

> A: $60,000
>
> B: $10,000
>
> C: $30,000

She looks at Santoso in disbelief. "You can't be serious," she says. "A is a lazy, aristocratic con man. And he is already rich—he doesn't need this money. It's C who made this profit for us really. And what about B—his plan was great, and what's more he can make better use of the bonus than anyone else? How can you possibly justify giving all that money to A?"

Santoso looks uneasy. He shrugs his shoulders. "A is a very important person," he says. "He is well-connected. Our company is lucky to have him. Without him there would be no project, no profit, and no bonus for anyone. If he finds out we paid the others more than him, he will be insulted. He may leave. And then where will we find such contracts? As for B, forget it. The family worries of others are no concern of ours."

Decision making is everyone's business. Each of us constantly makes decisions—which item on the menu to choose, which house to buy, whether or not to pursue a relationship. All the time, we choose from among alternatives. Mostly, we think we are doing so by being logical. We don't realize that it is often cultural patterns rather than logic that determine both the way we make decisions and the actual decisions we make. In the case above, Alice devised a very structured Western process for decision making, did her best to allocate fairly in relation to normal Western principles of rewarding effort and performance, but was probably influenced in her evaluation of B's reward by an ethic of humanitarianism. In contrast, Santoso wanted to discuss the problem before beginning to devise a solution, paid far more attention to role and status than to performance in making his allocation, and dismissed out of hand the humanitarian aspect for someone not part of his in-group. Alice and Santoso are adhering to decision models that are characteristic of their cultural backgrounds.

Culture influences what is perceived as desirable and also the appropriate way to achieve these goals. Because most decisions are complex, culture influences the way in which decision makers simplify the complex realty of decision making. If they are culturally intelligent, Santoso and Alice may be able to break out of their culturally based decision-making scripts and learn from each other.

The Rational Model

Decision making in many Western countries has been heavily influenced by the application of formal logic. This is particularly, and explicitly, true in the business sector, where companies succeed and fail according to their skills in making decisions about investments, business development, choice of market, choice of strategy, and many other factors. Because of the special importance of decision making in business settings, we use business examples as the basis for much of what we discuss in this chapter. But it is important to remember that culture influences all decision making, be it at work, in the home, or elsewhere.

The Western model tells us that decision making operates—or should operate—in a sequence of steps. Essentially these involve

- *defining a problem:* for example, a leadership vacuum created by the resignation of the organization's chief executive officer (CEO)
- *generating a range of potential solutions:* for example, attracting a range of candidates for the vacant CEO job
- *applying systematic analysis to the potential solutions to predict which one will best satisfy predetermined criteria:* for example, subjecting candidates to formal assessments in an attempt to determine which would provide the best leadership if appointed
- *choosing and implementing the best alternative:* for example, selecting, appointing, and supporting the candidate for CEO who performs best on the assessments[1]

This approach is the basis of management science and is implicit in the thinking behind such management decision-making techniques as linear programming, break-even analysis, feasibility studies, strategic choice, and personnel selection. Many managers pride themselves on their powers of reason and logic and typically promote and defend their decisions on this basis. However, other decision-making models are possible. What would you think of a board chair who said that the new CEO had been selected for one of the following reasons?

"His father had the job before him—it's a company tradition."

"We liked her more than any of the other candidates."

"He comes from a good family and attended an excellent university."

"We asked all the employees, and she got the most votes."

"We prayed, and God showed us the correct choice."

"We hired him because he is the brother of a board member."

"We all know him well, and we know we can trust him."

"Through his wife, he has excellent political connections."

"We chose her because she offered the biggest payment."

"I don't really know why we appointed him. It just seemed like the right thing to do. It was intuitive."

A board behaving in any of these ways in many Western countries might have its shareholders howling for blood. Yet in some parts of the world all of the criteria above are commonplace, understood, and part of the fabric of business decision making. Even in the West they may be more common than we imagine—it's just that it wouldn't do to admit to them. Instead, those who make an appointment based on tradition, personal attractiveness, family background, popularity, nepotism, friendship, politics, graft, or intuition typically deny that these factors have anything to do with it, and invent "rational" grounds for the decision.

This adherence to rational decision making—or at least a show of rational decision making—is of course part of a script or cultural cruise control as typically practiced by Westerners, which we have described previously in the book. In the case study with which we opened this chapter, rationality is part of the underlying philosophy of Alice Hughes. However, her Indonesian counterpart, Santoso, appears to be operating from different assumptions, with a script that elevates cultural norms and a political way of thinking about business above both rational decision making and concern for others. Cultures often have different criteria against which to assess decision outcomes.

Can Westerners be sure that the rational way of thinking in which they are indoctrinated by their society, their education, and their employing organizations is always the best basis for decision making? We think not. The world's diversity gives the West something to teach others about decision making and something to learn from others as well.

In this chapter we focus on the predominant rational model, indicate some limitations in its use, show some alternatives that are used effectively in other cultures, and advocate a more flexible, culturally intelligent approach to decision making based on appreciating and using a diversity of methods.

Problems with the Rational Model

Quite apart from the alternatives used in non-Western cultures, it is well known that the rational model of decision making is imperfect.[2] It might work well if

- decision makers had clear unambiguous criteria to work toward (for example, short-term versus long-term profit, market share, employee safety, family harmony, self-fulfillment). In fact, criteria are seldom clearly defined and often conflict with one another.

- decision makers were agreed on rational mental models to understand the human elements that are present in all human systems, including business organizations. It is often easy to understand a mechanical or financial system in rational terms, but in systems involving people, even highly qualified behavioral scientists can seldom agree.

- decision makers were capable of accurately defining the problem in the first place, generating a range of alternative solutions, accurately predicting the outcomes of all possible solutions, and manipulating huge amounts of relevant data. In fact, decision makers typically have limited capacity in the solutions they can generate, the predictions they can make, and the data they can handle. In the words of one management expert, much intended rational decision making gets replaced in practice by a much "messier" process of "muddling through."[3]

- decision makers were unbiased enough to stick with the solution suggested by a rational analysis, even if they personally didn't like it.

- there were time to consider fully every possible alternative. Imagine, for example, trying to select a new home by evaluating every single house in the city.

Even decision makers who pride themselves on their rationality are seldom able to overcome these difficulties. In practice, decision makers adopt various decision-making strategies that are less than rational. Here are some of the real methods that decision makers typically use to make their decisions:

- They work *incrementally,* moving gradually toward a decision in small steps rather than performing a single powerful analysis.

- They create *heuristics,* simple rules of thumb that may or may not have a rational basis but that simplify the decision-making task.[4]

- They *satisfice;* that is, they choose a plausible alternative that they become aware of early, rather than continuing to look for the best alternative.[5]

- They procrastinate, they panic, and sometimes they avoid the decision altogether.

These characteristics of the ways people make decisions are apparently consistent across cultures. Everyone simplifies the rational decision-making process in predictable ways. However, because individuals from different cultures have been programmed to see the world differently, they also differ in the ways they simplify the complex decision-making process.

For example, a common mental simplification or heuristic, called *availability*, is to rely on how easy it is to recall something from memory and to make judgments about its frequency, probability, or likely cause. That is, an event easily imagined is given more weight in making a judgment. Because this *heuristic* is based on experience, it can vary across cultures. For example, Thais would probably give a higher estimate than would Americans of the worldwide rate of death by being trampled by a water buffalo.

We have suggested that in some cultural settings decisions might be appropriate that are based not on rationality but on, say, tradition or consensus or family advantage or custom. Even if we can get around all the impediments to rationality mentioned above, what it means to be rational differs across cultures, and a decision made without reference to cultural factors is at least as likely to fail as a decision made purely on cultural grounds.

One reason why rational decisions fail to be made and implemented is the problem of acceptability. It has been wisely stated that the measure of a decision's adequacy is a function of its quality and its acceptability.[6] Trying to approximate rationality (appropriate definition of the problem, accurate information, and a logical process for analyzing it) will often give a high-quality result. For example, we may be able accurately to predict the sales and profitability of a new product line. But the decision not only has to be made, it also has to be *implemented,* usually by people other than the decision maker. In the case of the new product, the designers, product managers, marketers, and sales staff have to find the decision acceptable. And any couple who has tried to buy a new house knows that the most rational case in the world is useless against a statement such as "I just don't like the feel of it," and that living together successfully in a house depends on the house being acceptable to both partners. If the people involved do not accept the decision, they will not be committed to making the decision work, and, however rational it is, it is likely to fail. In the case with which we opened this chapter, Alice and Santoso need to work together toward a solution that they both find acceptable.

Culture imposes limits on what is acceptable and therefore on what decisions can realistically be implemented. In some countries the appointment of a woman to a high-status position—however well she may fit the criteria for the job—is unacceptable, so that even if the woman is appointed, she will most likely fail because of the unwillingness of those around her to work with her. In other countries the implementation of work practices and schedules that involve breaking religious taboos cannot be tolerated, no matter how rational they may be.

One of the most important limitations on rational decision making comes from the cultural dimension, identified in chapter 2, called *collectivism*. Collectivism calls into question not what the decision is but how the decision is made and who makes it. In an individualist culture, it is acceptable for an individual to make decisions, particularly if the society also has a norm of hierarchy and the decision maker has formal authority. But in a collectivist culture it is expected that the collective will be properly informed, consulted, and involved. Rational logic may be fine in a collectivist culture—provided everyone has the chance to contribute to the logic and to ponder and discuss whether it actually works.

We cannot emphasize strongly enough how important it is for Western decision makers to suspend, in part, their own belief in rationality as the basis for decision making and to be mindful of the specifics affecting decision making in other cultures. They may then be able to figure out how to reinterpret rationality to accommodate habits and constraints that are an important part of the local culture.

Motivation and Goals

In addition to the process of mental simplification described above, decisions are affected by the motives and goals of those who make them.[7] For example, a manager deciding whom to appoint as her assistant might be motivated by the desire to improve the organization's performance, the desire to remain popular with staff, the need to maintain power by appointing a weak subordinate, the wish to follow tradition, or any of a number of other factors. Such motives vary with culture. Individual needs reflect cultural values.

In many Western cultures, would-be rational decision makers pride themselves on their ability to set aside their personal motivations when they make decisions and to rely instead on applying logic to achieve the result that will be best for the company. Thus, they will choose the candidate they think will do the job best, rather than the one they like the most or the one who is a member of their family. The non-Western alternative to the rational model might be labeled the motivational model, in which individuals are, in a sense more honestly, driven by their own motives, values, traditions, and habits. These frequently have a cultural basis.

For example, the motivation for personal dominance and power is affected by the cultural dimension of power distance (chapter 2), which is high, for example, in Latin America but low in Scandinavian countries, Israel, and Australasia. Similarly, individualism (characteristic of the United States and many Western countries) is associated with need for achievement, while collectivism (characteristic of Latin America and many Asian countries) usually involves high need for affiliation (close personal relationships). Collectivism also reflects a worldview in which people are seen as interdependent with others, whereas in individualist cultures they are defined as independent.

A fundamental difference such as individualism-collectivism can dramatically affect business and political decisions. When British prime minister Margaret Thatcher famously remarked that "there is no such thing as society," she was making an exceptionally powerful statement of the individualist view at the heart of her attempts to foster a political and business system based on individual enterprise.

People from individualist cultures generally assert their own rights and ideas and resist group pressure, whereas those from collectivist cultures are more influenced by the context and the ideas of the other people involved. For example, in one research study,[8] people from collectivist Brazil were more likely than those from the individualist United States to forego a personal financial benefit in order to visit a sick friend. Another important product of individualism is high individual self-esteem and optimism. For example, Americans are much more likely to overestimate their abilities, chances of success, and so on than are the collectivist Japanese. But Japanese are more likely to believe that their judgments are shared by others.[9]

Culture also determines which decisions will be acceptable to people. Individual incentives for productivity may get good results in an individualist culture but not in a collectivist one. Participative group discussions about an issue by those involved in it may be irksome to those in an individualist culture because of the way the decision-making process is slowed down. In a high power-distance culture, people expect and may even welcome autocratic behavior from politicians, officials, and managers, but in a low power-distance culture, they will reject such behavior. Decision makers need to be mindful and have the skill to read the motivation of staff, particularly where that motivation is culturally based.

In addition, by considering culturally based motivational differences, people may be better able to understand the decision-making methods and criteria used by their counterparts with different cultural backgrounds. In the opening case in this chapter, Santoso and Alice are influenced by the collectivist and individualist natures of their respective cultures. Each acts according to the motivation of his or her cultural group. Both fail to exhibit cultural intelligence.

Selection and Allocation Decisions

IT'S WHO YOU KNOW THAT COUNTS

Jan Moore, the European area manager for Clarkson Equipment Corporation (CEC), was frustrated with the human resource management situation at CEC's joint venture in Russia. She contacted Craig Finley, CEC's country manager for Russia, to remind him that a human resource manager was supposed to have been hired three years ago, as soon as the joint venture was official. The Russian joint venture manager, Alexandr (Sasha) Lebedeva, had decided to manage the HR function himself.

As a result, all of the venture's senior managers had been appointed by the Russian partner. Additionally, quite a few of the senior managers' relatives had also been hired. The worst case, Jan believed, was that Sasha's son had already built an astonishing career within twelve months, starting as an assistant, becoming purchasing manager, and then being sent to Western Europe for eighteen months' practical training.

Unhappy with Sasha's hiring practices, Jan had instructed Craig to introduce CEC's standard hiring practices, which had been developed by the European headquarters. These included preparing job requisitions, advertising vacant positions, evaluating candidates' résumés, and having line managers conduct interviews. These had been introduced, but the Russian managers had ignored the procedures. For example, Jan discovered that just one week earlier a new machine operator had been hired for the factory without Craig's knowledge. He turned out to be the inexperienced eighteen-year-old son of a local customs officer who often cleared shipments for CEC.

When Jan confronted Craig about the matter, she got a rather philosophical reply: "Well, you have to remember the specifics of the country you are operating in. Russia has an Asian culture, and European faces should not mislead you. Western standards do not always work here. If hiring people you have known for a long time and therefore trust is a local custom, you can't change it overnight. And you probably don't need to change it."[10]

Staff selection decisions are among the most common decisions in organizations. In the example, the Westerners, as usual, propose a rational model in the assessment of candidates, focusing on behavior. The Russians prefer to rely on more subtle and traditional cues of suitability for the job.

One way of understanding these differences is to contrast the Western view that what counts is *what you can do* with the Eastern belief that it is *who you are* that matters. In our initial case, Santoso's awarding of most of the bonus to the person with the highest status and the most critical role rather than to the biggest contributor is a case in point. In China, the network of a candidate's relationships, his or her *guanxi*,[11] can be critical to selection for a job. *Guanxi*, though, is more complex and subtle than a simple relationship. It is likely to exist as part of a network of family and personal connections and to involve delicate patterns of mutual obligation.

In the West, this kind of thing is thought of as favoritism or nepotism and is frowned upon: rather than relying on their connections, candidates are expected to demonstrate their personal suitability for the job. The East-West difference may be made worse by the current Western fashion—often built into local legislation—for equal employment opportunity, meaning opportunity based solely on the Western criterion of individually demonstrated ability to do the job.

Other cultural differences in selection practice are more subtle. In one recent research study conducted in Europe,[12] the ability to do the job was the main criterion across a number of countries, but "ability" was very differently defined, with egalitarian Scandinavian countries putting a lot of emphasis on interpersonal skills, whereas countries emphasizing status differences paid more attention to age.

Reward allocation decisions such as that in the opening case in this chapter require the making of decisions that balance equality against equity. Suppose several people collaborate to complete a project, but some use more skill, work longer hours, and make more effort than others. An equitable allocation will distribute rewards in relation to responsibility, time, effort, and so on. An equal allocation will reward all participants equally just for contributing. Individualist cultures generally favor equitable solutions, and collectivist cultures in some cases favor equal ones. Collectivists are also more likely to take into account need as a criterion for reward allocation.

Ethics and Decision Making

THE TRADE PERMIT

Mohammed is an immigration official in a Middle Eastern country. One of his jobs is to review applications for trading permits issued to overseas visitors. He has to ensure that all the appropriate criteria are met. If they are, he will normally grant the permit.

Mohammed's salary for this job is extremely low. Relying on his salary alone, Mohammed would find it very difficult to provide even the bare essentials for his family. Fortunately there is relief for him in the system: he is good at his job, and it is customary for applicants to show their appreciation for his service by giving him small sums of money. Some of these applicants are Americans and Europeans from wealthy multinational companies, which can easily afford these additional costs. The arrangement is well understood by nearly everyone in Mohammed's country and works to the advantage of all.

Recently, however, Mohammed has had some difficulty working with a man called John O'Connell, who has recently arrived as the sole trade representative for an Irish company seeking to build an export-import business. O'Connell is well dressed and formal. When he presented his application, it was impeccable. However, he showed no signs of offering a financial accommodation. Perhaps, Mohammed thought, this was just an oversight. Perhaps Mr. O'Connell did not realize how much authority Mohammed had in this situation. He told him that there was some further paperwork to be done and that he should come back in a few days.

O'Connell has been back twice. On each occasion he has become more irritated at the delays, but despite some broad hints dropped by Mohammed, he still has not offered any cash. So Mohammed continues to prevaricate: if Mr. O'Connell will not play the game according to the established rules, he will have to accept the consequences.

Back at his office, John O'Connell calls an old friend in Ireland, a man with experience in the country in question. The friend immediately realizes what the problem is and advises John how much he should offer and how he should make the offer. John becomes angry.

"But that's bribery!" he exclaims, "Pure corruption."

"No, it's just the way these people do things," says the friend. "Think of it as a tip."

In the global business environment and generally in life virtually every decision has an ethical component. The business and political press regularly tell us of ongoing ethical crises in many countries: for example, a continuing flow of politicians and business executives lining their pockets through the pillaging of their countries and companies; lies and deception practiced against shareholders; "pork-barrel" politics; systematic bribery and corruption in governmental institutions; embezzlement, credit card and computer fraud. But what is ethical and what is not is not always clear-cut, and in particular different societies often have very different views of what behavior is morally unacceptable. Monetary payoffs to officials in return for favors granted—the essence of the above case—represent just such an issue. The following are examples of common business decisions that present global organizations with ethical dilemmas:

- Moving production to a foreign country to take advantage of cheap labor, resulting in obvious exploitation and dangerous working conditions.

- Discouraging union organizing in countries where unions are not well established.

- Abiding only by the minimum environmental protection laws imposed by the country in which the company is operating, standards that may be much lower than those in the company's own culture.

- Promoting dangerous products (such as cigarettes) in a foreign market when demand declines at home.

- Doing business in a country with a repressive government.

- Exporting harmful substances that are illegal in a company's home country but not in the host country.

- Imposing a global ethical norm developed by the headquarters of the firm.

- Advertising luxury goods in less developed countries.

However, you don't have to be at the top of the organization, or even in an organization, to face ethical dilemmas in your decision making. Whether to pay unofficial inducements, what level of expenses to claim, whether to accept gifts from prospective suppliers, how much to claim on your theft insurance when your house is burgled—all these issues raise ethical questions. Those doing business internationally or dealing with staff or colleagues from different cultures quickly realize that what they think is morally correct erodes in the face of differing cultural values and norms for behavior. They often have difficulty reconciling their own ethical standards with local practices, and they often have great difficulty, when invited to do something they truly believe to be wrong, to say no.

The reason these are difficulties is that many business decisions are ethically ambiguous. Consider the common decision of firms in economically advanced countries to relocate manufacturing in developing countries in order to achieve lower labor costs. Here is how such a decision might be perceived by (a) a manager from a developed country making such a decision in order to keep his company in business and (b) an activist concerned about the welfare of the people in the developing world.

> Businessman: "If we do not make this decision, we will go out of business, and everyone will lose their jobs, not just those in our European factory. We would be bringing to the people of the region in China where we seek to set up our factory an opportunity to participate in the Western dream of secure employment. We will pay a competitive wage to attract their labor. No one will force anybody to work for us—they will do it because they know they are better off that way. We are helping them! But we cannot pay more. That would enable our competitors to take our market away, and everyone would suffer, including our Chinese employees. Our extension to China, you see, is totally ethical."

> Activist: "Your company is a fundamentally immoral organization, interested only in generating huge profits for its managers and shareholders. It seeks to move into China only because it knows it can exploit the people there. It will pay them wages that they can scarcely live on, force them to work long hours, and neglect their health and safety needs. If the company really wants to help the Chinese people, why doesn't it double the proposed wages and ensure reasonable working conditions? It could do that and still make a huge profit. But multinationals don't think this way because they are fundamentally unethical."

Who is right? Both! The two protagonists are proceeding from very different frames of reference. Interestingly, though, each party is seeking to do right by the Chinese workers involved.

To the activist, the concept of profit appears inherently immoral. Her questioning is part of a radical analysis of "big business" that focuses particularly on multinational companies because they use intercountry differences in areas such as labor costs, pollution control, and ability to get their way with government authorities as a basis for making big decisions—such as relocation—in the "rational" interest of profitability. This basis is part of a wider belief by businesspeople that in the end striving for profit is good for everyone—including the Chinese workers—because it causes economic systems to become more and more efficient and makes goods cheaper. While different cultures tend to have different views of business freedom and control, the moral questions separating the businessman in our example from the activist cut across cultural boundaries, and the attitudes and institutions that support them are international.

The situation described above represents perhaps the most difficult ethical dilemma that global managers face. It is essentially the question "Should I follow a practice that is allowed in a foreign country but not in my own?" Managers commonly try to answer this question in three ways.[13]

- The first of these tries to evaluate the consequences of the decision and calculate the maximum benefit for the most people. This is what the businessman was arguing in defense of moving his factory to China. Many Chinese people would benefit, as well as the businessman's own shareholders. However, as indicated by the response of the activist, benefit is often in the eye of the beholder.

- The second approach is to rely on some moral rule. We all learn such rules as part of our cultural socialization, and these rules are often apparent in religious teachings. An example is the idea of treating others as you would like to be treated. However, the obvious problem with moral rules is finding a set of rules upon which all cultures can agree. For example, even in cultures as similar as the United States and Canada, strong differences in opinion exist with regard to the right of the state to put someone to death.

- The final method of answering ethical questions is the culturally relative approach. This approach suggests that ethical behavior varies from one culture to the next. While seemingly consistent with our general recommendations for being culturally intelligent, this approach is also insufficient to deal with the ethical dilemmas of global managers attempting to make decisions across cultural boundaries. While many differences in business practice are in fact related to the cultural norms of a society, cultural relativity can make it possible for people to justify truly reprehensible behavior based on culture.

What then is the individual who wants to make an ethical decision to do? Not surprisingly, we suggest that the steps to cultural intelligence will also lead to more ethical decision making across cultures.

The first step is *knowledge*. We need to understand our own mental programming with regard to what is ethical. What do we believe is proper behavior and why do we believe it? We also need an awareness that people in other cultures hold a variety of values that are relative to their society.

The second step is being *mindful* of the ethical component of decisions. Who is likely to benefit, and who will be harmed by the decision? In this case, mindfulness also means paying attention to all the factors that might influence the decision. These include the relative level of economic development in a society. The mindful decision maker will ask, "Would this practice be acceptable in my country at a similar level of economic development? Is this practice a violation of some fundamental human right?"[14]

The cross-cultural *skills* of the culturally intelligent decision maker will include a repertoire of behaviors that recognize value differences across cultures but are consistent with self-chosen ethical principles. These principles will develop over time as the individual gains more knowledge and practices mindfulness. He or she will uphold these nonrelative values and rights regardless of majority opinion and will act in accord with these principles. Doing so will often require creative solutions to ethical dilemmas. For example, one organization, while yielding to the cultural norm of employing children under the age of fifteen in its manufacturing process in a developing country, also provided time off and monetary support to allow these children to acquire a basic education.

Summary

This chapter describes decision making in cross-cultural context. It may be that the world is gradually accepting a Western-style rational approach to decision making, but this approach is far from universal. Globalization is itself a strategy that is driven by a relentless logic of business profitability, and the process of globalization has been led and dominated by organizations based in the United States and Western European countries attempting to impose that logic in Latin America, Asia, Eastern Europe, and the Middle East. However, because people in different cultures have different mental programming, the ways in which they simplify the complex process of decision making also differ. Even in attempting a rational process, the ways they define a problem and generate, weight, and select alternatives are likely to be different. Also, decisions are affected by the motives and goals of the decision maker, which are based on culturally different values. The culturally intelligent person is better able to understand the decision-making methods and criteria used in other cultures. Virtually all decisions have an ethical component because some stakeholders benefit and others do not. The culturally intelligent decision maker is able to balance the culturally relative nature of ethics while upholding fundamental human rights.

CHAPTER 5

Communicating, Negotiating, and Resolving Conflicts across Cultures

COMMUNICATION FAILURE

Consider these four vignettes of cross-cultural living, all of them authentic experiences involving Americans.[1]

- An Australian woman, flying aboard Sky West Airlines from Atlanta to Pittsburgh, asks a flight attendant if she can have a pack of pretzels instead of crackers. When the attendant says they don't have any pretzels, she replies, "Fair dinkum?" But before the Australian can say anything more, a second attendant asks for her passport and copies down her name. Her local colloquialism has sparked a security scare, her common Australian phrase apparently being misinterpreted as an act of aggression.

- An American student shares a dormitory room with a Thai. They get on well. Then, after they have lived together for several weeks, the Thai abruptly announces that he has applied for a transfer to another room. The American is surprised and upset and asks the Thai why he wants to move. The Thai is reluctant to speak but eventually says that he can't stand the American's noisiness, loud stereo, late visitors, and untidiness. The American is even more surprised: all this is new to him. "Couldn't you have told me this sooner?" he says. "Maybe I could have done something about it."

- A newly qualified American community counselor is assigned as a client a Malaysian man who suffers from low energy and poor concentration. In their first interview, the Malaysian is very quiet and withdrawn. The counselor is used to silences in counseling sessions, as clients reflect and analyze, but this client does not seem to want to communicate at all. So the counselor takes time to try to persuade him of the nature of the counseling process. At the end of the session, the client does not seek any further counseling. The counselor is disappointed: he has learned almost nothing about his client. Has he done something wrong?

- An American economist is on a study tour in China. He visits an economic planning institute where a Chinese economist, who is interested in the American's economic forecasting techniques, invites him to spend two months in China giving seminars. The American is very interested in the offer, and says so, but he adds that he has to check with the administration of his U.S. institute to get their approval. Back in the United States, he is granted the necessary clearance and sends a message to China indicating that he is definitely available. But the Chinese never contact him again.

These cases, to which we will return later, demonstrate communication failures that led to the breakdown of relationships, and all have cultural origins.

Communication—the interchange of messages between people—is the fundamental building block of social experience. Whether selling, buying, negotiating, leading, or working with others, we communicate. And although the idea of communicating a message seems simple and straightforward—"You just tell it straight. And you listen."—when it comes to figuring out what goes wrong in life, "communication failure" is by far the most common explanation.

Communication operates through *codes*—systems of signs in which each sign signifies a particular idea. Communication also uses *conventions*—agreed-upon norms about how, when, and in what context codes will be used. If two people do not share the same codes and conventions, they will have difficulty communicating with each other. And codes and conventions are determined mainly by people's cultures. The most obvious example of unshared codes is different languages.

Each communication breakdown in our opening set of vignettes can be explained in terms of cultural differences:

- In the first case the expression "fair dinkum" is a common Australian phrase that is used to refer to something worthwhile or reliable. As a question, it can mean "Really? Is that right?" and this is most likely the sense in which the passenger used it. However this term was not in the vocabulary of the American flight attendants. And they drew a wrong conclusion. This is an example of different *codes*.

- In the case of the student whose Thai friend moved out, culture and custom interfered with communication. In their upbringing, Americans are encouraged to be active, assertive, and open, and to expect the same in others. In *their* upbringing, Thais are encouraged to be passive and sensitive, and they too expect the same in others. The Thai expected the American to be sensitive to his feelings; the American expected the Thai to say what his feelings were. When neither behaved as expected, the relationship broke down. This is an example of different *conventions*.

- The counselor whose client wouldn't talk failed to appreciate the meaning of an important part of the communication—the silences! Silences are not always absence of communication; they are often *part* of communication. Asians tend to wait longer than Westerners before speaking, especially to authority figures. To some extent long silences are a sign of respect. The counselor might have been more patient. Also, the Malaysian may not have been assertive enough to seek another appointment without being invited. So the whole situation was mismanaged. This is an example of different *codes* AND *conventions*.

- The economist whose invitation to visit China was never followed up failed to appreciate the meaning of his own communication in Chinese culture. A Chinese saying that he had to check with his office before accepting the invitation might have been communicating two things: first, that he was a relatively low-status person who had to check everything with bureaucrats; second, that he was not really interested in visiting. So in this case the Chinese may have made these same assumptions about the American and concluded he was not really interested in visiting. Chinese people seldom say "no" even when that is what they mean. Instead, they have numerous polite ways—including the one in this story—of courteously indicating it. This is another example of different *codes* AND *conventions*.

How Cross-Cultural Communication Works

In communication, the communicator transmits messages to others ("receivers") who interpret them. The process is shown in figure 5.1.

When the receiver in turn becomes the communicator, the process is reversed. The channel may be spoken words, written words, or nonverbal behavior such as gestures or facial expressions. Face-to-face conversations, meetings, telephone calls, documents, or e-mails may all be used. Successful communication occurs when the message is accurately perceived and understood. Skills of communicating and listening, selection of an appropriate channel, and the absence of "interference" from external factors are all important. Cultural differences threaten communication because they reduce the available codes and conventions that are shared by sender and receiver.

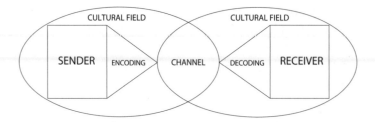

FIGURE 5.1. Cross-cultural communication process
Source: Based on Schramm (1980)

The cultural field shown in figure 5.1 represents culturally based elements in the sender's and in the receiver's background, such as their language, education, and values.[2] The cultural field creates the codes and conventions that affect the communication process.

Language

Language is the most obvious code for communicating. In language, combinations of sounds represent elements of meaning and can be combined to represent complex messages. Most languages contain speech conventions, subtleties, and figures of speech of which only experienced speakers may be aware.

The essence of language is that sender and receiver should share the code. But the development and mobility of humankind has left us with thousands of different languages, plus different dialects and adaptations of many of them.[3] Most people have only one language, which they have learned and spoken since early childhood, and even accomplished linguists are usually fluent in only a few. Moreover, psychologists have determined that the best time to acquire new languages is before the age of ten, after which we become progressively less able to adapt.[4]

A complicating factor is that whatever the language, its

everyday use normally goes beyond any simple single code such as that in a dictionary. Languages are living entities that grow and change to accommodate the widely different groups who use them and the changes in the social circumstances in which they are used. For example, among young speakers of English, language is becoming more direct and dramatic, so that

> "She accused me of breaking the window. I said I hadn't."

has become:

> "She's like, 'You trashed the window!' I'm like, 'No way it was me!'"

In most cultures, different groups have their own vocabularies, slang, accents, and idioms. Sometimes the differences are so strong and systematic that we say they have a different dialect. Technical or social groups may develop their own jargon and may use the jargon to distance themselves from outsiders. Another common linguistic convention is euphemism, when words with sexual or other potentially impolite connotations are replaced with less explicit words. For example, in some English-speaking cultures it is common to say that someone has "passed away" rather than "died."

Finally, most of us would be surprised at the extent to which we mindlessly use proverbs, maxims, and even slogans or catchphrases heard on television as part of our day-to-day conversation. Examples are the Anglo-American expressions "it's a no-brainer," "yadda yadda yadda," and "it's not rocket science." Such expressions are in good English but may genuinely puzzle outsiders.

Finding Common Language Codes

While language is a wonderful tool for communication, it is also fraught with difficulties. Two people seeking to communicate with each other who do not have any overlapping language codes face a major barrier. They can, of course, employ translators. But translation is time-consuming and expensive. It also complicates the communication process and potentially distorts the message by requiring a further transformation.

People who choose to learn and use a foreign language find benefits beyond simply overcoming the language barrier. Most people appreciate the efforts that others may have made to learn their language. So even though your fluency in another language may be limited, the fact that you have made the effort may generate goodwill.[5] In addition, language conveys many subtleties about a culture that a person with high cultural intelligence might notice and use.

However, learning a new language carries major costs. Becoming fluent in another language takes substantial study and practice, particularly if that language is unlike your own in pronunciation, grammar, and conventions. Language learners expend considerable time and effort in learning, and find that when using the language they feel stressed and may even be distracted from other aspects of the situation. Also, lack of fluency may unfairly undermine credibility in the eyes of fluent speakers. In contrast, fluency may lead to the speaker being perceived, sometimes mistakenly, as being competent in other areas, such as overall cultural intelligence.[6]

Second-Language Use

One by-product of the Anglo-American economic dominance of the twentieth century and the relentless unwillingness of British and American people to learn languages other than their own has been to make English increasingly the accepted common language of business. Worldwide, the learning of English to facilitate international communication has become a major activity. This change facilitates international business communication. Those who speak English as their only language owe a debt to the millions of people around the world who have gone out of their way to learn to understand, read, speak, and write in the English language.

Learning English as a second language (ESL) is full of challenges. The language's richness of vocabulary and its numerous synonyms can cause ESL speakers great difficulty. Take the simple word "fly." It can mean an annoying insect, a means of travel, or an important part of men's trousers.[7]

A person fluent in English who is communicating with a less skilled English speaker has an obligation to communicate in relatively standard terms, to avoid jargon and obscure language, and to avoid assumptions about comprehension by the other person. Culturally intelligent people will consciously adapt their language to be in harmony with the vocabulary and style of the other person.

Some ESL speakers—particularly those from cultures that set high store by not losing face—pretend to understand when they really do not. In these situations there is a special onus on the parties to be aware of barriers and limitations in their sending and receiving, and to check whether messages have successfully gotten through.

The following are some brief guidelines that culturally intelligent people can use to help improve communication with ESL speakers.

Second-Language Strategies

- Enunciate carefully.
- Avoid colloquial expressions.
- Repeat important points using different words to explain the same concept.
- Use active verbs and avoid long compound sentences.
- Use visual restatements such as pictures, graphs, tables, and slides.
- Hand out written summaries of your verbal presentation.
- Pause more frequently, and do not jump in to fill silences.

- Take frequent breaks, and allow more time.

- Do not attribute poor grammar or mispronunciation to lack of intelligence.

- Check for understanding by encouraging speakers to repeat concepts back to you.

- Avoid embarrassing speakers, but encourage and reinforce their participation.[8]

Conventions

Communication conventions cover the ways that language and other codes are used within a particular culture. Once again, cultural values and norms, such as those based on collectivism or individualism, are apparent.

EXPLICIT AND IMPLICIT COMMUNICATION

There is a Western view that individuals perceive something called the truth and should state it, and a convention that communication should be verbal and that verbal messages should be explicit, direct, and unambiguous. But in other cultures—for example, many Middle Eastern and Asian cultures—there is no absolute truth, and politeness and desire to avoid embarrassment often take precedence. The convention is therefore that communication is implicit and indirect. In the direct convention of communication, most of the message is placed in the *content* of the communication—the words that are used. In the indirect convention, the *context* is more important—for example, the physical setting, the previous relationships between the participants, and the nonverbal behavior of those involved.

The direct convention tends to be the norm in countries with individualist cultures, the indirect in countries with collectivist cultures. Understanding apparently indirect communication in collectivist cultures may sometimes be simply a matter of learning another code. The examples in the following box show a variety of ways of saying no politely and indirectly. In most cases a low-CQ individual would understandably think that the answer might be "yes."

Conditional "yes"	If everything proceeds as planned, the proposal will be approved.
Counter-question	Have you submitted a copy of your proposal to the ministry of . . . ?
Criticizing the question	Your question is very difficult to answer.
Refusing the question	We cannot answer this question at this time.
Tangential reply	Will you be staying longer than you had originally planned?
Yes, but	Yes, approval looks likely, but . . .
Delayed answer	You should know shortly.

The problems associated with explicitness of communication are not limited to face-to-face communication. In fact, the use of e-mail as the preferred mode of communication in many firms can make these problems even more difficult. One Dutch manager (direct convention) was so frustrated in trying to understand the real message in e-mails from his Mexican counterpart (indirect convention) that he finally jumped on an airplane and flew from Amsterdam to Mexico City just to get clarification.[10]

VERBOSITY AND SILENCE

Cultures vary in their conventions about *how much* and *how loudly* one should talk. Americans are notorious for talking a lot and talking loudly. Silence can be used deliberately and strategically in communication. Japanese negotiators use silence as a means of controlling negotiating processes, whereas Finns use it as a way of encouraging a speaker to continue. As the counselor in one of our opening vignettes failed to note, in Malaysia silence can show respect. Interpreting silence accurately is important in culturally intelligent communication.

Nonverbal Communication

RAY MOVES TO GREECE

I had no trouble finding the café. It was picture-perfect, as many are in Athens: checkered tablecloths, white walls, nice Mediterranean atmosphere. It was morning, so there were no customers. Behind the counter, a slim woman in her forties was getting ready for the start of the day. Dimitri's mother. I'd seen her photos.

"Mrs. Theodoridis?"

She turned toward me, puzzled.

"I'm Ray. From Australia. Your son Dimitri . . . "

She smiled broadly. "Oh, Ray! Yes! You Ray! Oh yes, Dimitri write me that you come to Greece. Oh, come, come! Sit! I bring you come coffee."

She moved toward the kitchen, motioning me to sit at one of the tables. Suddenly, a worried frown spread across her features. "Oh! Maybe you no like Greek coffee? Maybe you want ouzo?"

She was fussing over me. If there's one thing we Australians can't stand, it's being fussed over. But I stayed polite.

"Coffee would be great, thank you."

She nodded and went into the kitchen. I sat down at the table. She came back with the coffee and stood opposite me. She was speaking to me in a warm, indulgent gush.

"Dimitri tell me you *so* help him when he move to Australia, with his English and everything." She put the coffee down on the table and sat down opposite me, leaning toward me. She seemed too close. I could smell her perfume. I leaned back a little. Australian guys don't like being gushed over; we like to keep our distance.

"So." Suddenly she placed both her hands over one of mine, flat on the table. She stroked my hand a little. "How you like Athens?" Before I could answer, she moved her right hand, took a gentle hold of my cheek, and shook it affectionately. "You find girlfriend, yes?"

This was not going the way I had expected. I had envisaged a more formal conversation, at a respectable distance, about Dimitri. Instead she had her hands all over me. Her eyes seemed to be staring right through me. And she was asking about my love life, for heaven's sake! What business was it of hers?

"Well, Mrs. Theodoridis," I managed, "I . . . err . . . um . . ." She was leaning toward me, close, intense. "I've only been here a couple of months."

"Yes, Ray, that's right." She was speaking to me as to a ten-year-old child. Now she took my face in both her hands, and leaned even closer. "You find nice Greek girl, settle down." At last she took her hands off me and leaned back, considering. "Some nice Greek girls. You have good salary at Constantine Shipping, yes?" She sipped her coffee. I was thinking, what *is* it with this woman? She is altogether too familiar. Better be polite, though.

"Well, Mrs. Theodoridis, I . . . err . . . haven't really thought about settling down."

"Yes, Ray, that's right." Why was she agreeing with everything I said? "Better be careful. Some of these Greek girls, they want big diamond ring, or fancy church wedding." A thought occurred to her. She leaned toward me, put her hand under my chin, and looked at me intensely. She said softly "Are you religious, Ray?"

Bugger me, I thought, I've only known her two minutes, and already she's asking about my personal life, my money, and my religion! I felt confused, embarrassed, and hot. And her constant pawing was getting to me. What to do?

Then I had a brainwave. Play for time! "Ah, well, Mrs. Theodoridis. Maybe I will have that ouzo after all."

"Aah!" She smiled and grasped my hand in a way that said, this is our special, shared moment. Then she got up, ruffled my hair, and went into the kitchen.

I looked after her, shaking my head involuntarily. What was she about? Why was she so personal to a stranger, why so intimate? What did she *want*?

This case is a good example of poor communication due to cultural differences in conventions and body language. Greece is a collectivist culture, with a lot of emphasis on the extended family. Mrs. Theodoridis is treating Ray like a member of that family because of his close relationship to her son Dimitri— indeed she is treating him as if he *is* her son. And like many people in Southern European cultures, Greek people have a low interpersonal distance, and touching of the type Mrs. Theodoridis is doing is not uncommon, particularly between members of the extended family. But Ray, from the more reserved, higher-distance Australian culture, sees all this as intrusive: in his culture, touching between men and women often has sexual connotations. No wonder he is confused! And, it has to be said, in failing to notice Ray's embarrassment Mrs. Theodoridis shows low cultural intelligence.

The topic of body language is popular, and most of us now realize that we communicate, often inadvertently, by such means as physical proximity and orientation to another person, body movements, gestures, facial expression, eye contact, and tone of voice. Thus, nonverbal communication supplements verbal communication a great deal.

Often, nonverbal communication is a good guide to the truth: for example, if an athlete is sitting in the dressing room after the match with shoulders slumped, arms folded, and face glum, you do not need to ask, whatever his or her culture, whether his team won or lost. Sometimes nonverbal behavior reveals the opposite of verbal, for example, when someone red in the face and making a considerable effort to control himself, tells you, "No, I'm *not* angry."

Nonverbal communication often assists cross-cultural understanding because many nonverbal signals are similar between different cultures. For example, smiling universally expresses positive feelings. But there are also subtle variations between cultures: for example, Asians often smile to conceal nervousness or embarrassment. A shake of the head means disagreement in Western cultures but agreement in some parts of India. The codes that tell us the meanings of postures or gestures, or where to stand or whether to bow, sometimes agree across cultures but sometimes disagree.

DISTANCE

How close should you stand to other people when communicating with them? Should you face people directly or stand beside them? The answer can vary according to the characteristics of the other person, for example, his or her authority, age, or gender. But there are also differences among cultures. For example, in casual conversation, Greeks stand closer than Americans, who stand closer than Norwegians, and so on. A culturally intelligent person will be mindful of the comfort of those he or she deals with and will modify his or her social distance.[11]

TOUCHING

Should you ever touch the person you are communicating with? If so, where, and how much? In most cultures, touching another person symbolizes various emotions and relationships. The most obvious example is the handshake, which in many cultures denotes a friendly relationship—"I'm pleased to meet you" or "Goodbye for now." Kissing another person's cheek is common between men as well as women in France. In some cultures, approval or support may be shown by a slap on the back or a squeeze of the arm. Soccer players worldwide hug each other fiercely when their team scores a goal.

Because of gender differences and concerns about the sexual connotations of touching, conventions are often different for men and women. There are low-touch cultures (predominantly in North America, Northern Europe, and Asia) and high-touch cultures (predominantly in Latin America, Southern and Eastern Europe, and the Middle East). A touch that is meant to be meaningful in the United States, such as a pat on the back, might not even be noticed in a high-touch culture like Brazil.

BODY POSITION

In a case in chapter 1, a Samoan job applicant sat down in the office of an American manager to show respect by positioning himself at a physically lower level. But the gesture misfired because to Americans sitting down when others are standing shows disrespect. Polite Americans wait for others to sit down before they do, and show respect by rising from their seats when others enter the room. The way people position themselves has meaning in all cultures, but it is hard to draw up any hard-and-fast rules.

Another common body-position issue is the adoption of a position that makes one's body look big—for example a rigid, angular stance to denote aggression or a curled-up, cowering posture to indicate submissiveness.[12] Bowing to show deference is common across many cultures, but in some its use is extreme. In Japan, the (unwritten) rules about who should bow to whom and how exactly they should do it are complex, subtle, and difficult to master. In fact, the culturally intelligent person knows that a foreigner trying to imitate Japanese bowing is at best humorous and at worst offensive, and that bowing in Japan is a custom best reserved for native Japanese.

GESTURES

Hand and arm movements are often used simply as physical accompaniments to words, to supplement them or to provide a visual illustration. Often gestures are meaningless without the verbal commentary, other than as a general statement of the state of mind of the person. But there are also gestures that carry established meanings, for example pointing to indicate direction, hands held up with the palms facing upward and outward to indicate defensiveness, and a shrug of the shoulders to indicate incomprehension or lack of interest. Other signals vary across cultures. Some gestures, which are positive, humorous, or harmless in some cultures, are considered hostile, offensive, or obscene in other cultures. High-CQ people tend to avoid explicit gestures until they know what they mean.

FACIAL EXPRESSION

Facial expressions most obviously indicate the basic human emotions: happiness, surprise, disgust, fear, anger, and sadness. The facial expressions denoting these are instinctive and common across cultures.[13] However, in most cultures people have learned how to disguise their emotions by adopting an expression that does not represent how they really feel. For example, do you truly believe that the flight attendant beaming happily at every passenger she serves is truly happy to meet each one? In some Asian cultures, smiling is often used to hide displeasure, sadness, or anger.

Emotions can also be concealed by the adoption of a neutral expression. Every negotiator and card player knows the value of being able to sit with a face devoid of any expression that might indicate to others how he or she is feeling. Thus, while natural facial expressions provide a cross-cultural *code* to others' emotions, in many situations *conventions* can mean that facial cues are either absent or misleading. For example, in collectivist cultures, the open expression of individual emotion is often suppressed because it may threaten group harmony. This is one reason why Westerners often characterize Chinese and Japanese people as inscrutable.

EYE CONTACT

Making, or avoiding, eye contact is another important form of nonverbal communication. In Western countries a moderate level of eye contact during conversation is a way of communicating friendliness or interest, whereas excessive eye contact (staring) is considered rude and lack of eye contact can be perceived as hostile. Eye contact is also used in conversation as a signal: for example, making eye contact with the other person as you finish a sentence often means, "Now it's your turn to speak." But Arabs, Latinos, Indians, and Pakistanis all have conventions of longer eye contact, whereas Africans and East Asians interpret eye contact as conveying anger or insubordination. A further complication is the fact that most cultures have different conventions about eye contact depending on the gender, status, and so on of those involved.

With all areas of nonverbal communication, the ability to observe the behavior of others, to be mindful of it, and to be skilled at modifying one's own behavior are key components of cultural intelligence.

Negotiating across Cultures

Negotiation is a special communication situation in which the objective is often for people to overcome conflicting interests and to reach an agreement that is advantageous to all. The practices of negotiation include the making of threats and promises, the use of persuasion, the signaling of concessions, and the development of compromises and creative solutions. As usual, the existence of cross-cultural differences complicates things. Most international tourists know, for example, that there are some countries in which it is accepted custom to haggle in shops over the price of souvenirs, and others where one is expected to pay the marked price without any fuss.

WHEN IS IT TIME TO DO BUSINESS?

Bill Miller, a top American salesman with a major information technology manufacturer, sits in his Mexico City hotel room, head bowed, running his hands through his hair in frustration. Two days into his trip and with only twenty-four hours left, he feels he is no closer to "closing" the sale he is trying to make than he was when he arrived.

It's not that his Mexican hosts are hostile. On the contrary, they smile broadly at him, take a personal interest in him, and certainly look after all his physical needs: the hotel, for example, is excellent. But the Mexicans show very little interest in talking business. The manager who has been assigned to look after Bill is a good host but is not party to the deal Bill wants to negotiate. On the way in from the airport, when Bill began to talk about his carefully prepared sales presentation, the manager seemed surprised. "Plenty of time for that later," he advised. "For the moment, you must be tired from your flight. Why not relax for a day or two and do some sightseeing first? I can look after you."

So Bill spent his first day being shown around Mexico City, struggling to conceal his impatience. On the second day, however, his host invited him to an after-work meeting with the senior managers of the company. Bill prepared carefully and arrived promptly at the meeting room with his PowerPoint display. No one was there, just a table of drinks and nibbles. Gradually the executives drifted in. They engaged Bill conversationally in English and began to ask questions. But the questions were not about the equipment Bill had to sell but about his company—its history, its plans, and its future expansion in Latin America. Next, they moved on to Bill himself, his history in the company, his views of the IT industry and their own industry, even his wife, family, and hobbies.

Bill was still impatient. He wanted to get on with his presentation, but he did not want to offend his hosts. Eventually, during a pause, he said, "Thanks—I am so grateful for your hospitality. Now, I wonder if we might sit down and let me go through my presentation. I think we have a real good deal here for your company."

There was an embarrassed silence. Then the deputy CEO said slowly, "Unfortunately, I think Mr. Alvarez may already have gone home." Alvarez was the CEO, and without his signature there could be no deal. "Maybe . . ." said the deputy CEO, "maybe tomorrow? In the meantime, why not come out to dinner so we can get to know each other better?" This time, Bill pleaded fatigue.

How on earth, he wondered, did these people ever sell anything to each other, or buy anything from each other, let alone from him?

Back at his home, Juan Alvarez lit a cigarette thoughtfully. The American had looked so ill at ease that Juan just hadn't felt like sticking around. He had wanted to try to build a business relationship, a basis not just for one future deal, but for many. Miller had thrown it back in his face. Alvarez had seen it before with Americans.

How on earth, he wondered, did they ever learn to really trust each other in business?

The behavior of the different participants in the story and the reflections of Miller and Alvarez reveal distinct outlooks on business relationships and how best to pursue them. Bill, like most Americans, is concerned with the short term, with being efficient, reaching a conclusion, and not wasting time on social trivia. Juan and his staff, like members of most Latin cultures and many others, believe that good business is the result of good business relationships. Therefore, the initial effort must go into building a relationship: it is worth spending time to do so.

The result is that both Bill and Juan endanger what they value most—Bill endangers the immediate transaction, and Juan endangers the long-term business relationship. If each had been willing to accommodate, at least in part, the other's customs, a worthwhile business relationship could by now be under way and each could have secured exactly what he wanted.

Negotiating Styles

Negotiation processes typically go through different phases, and there are intercultural differences in the emphasis on each phase. The phases are:

- building a relationship
- exchanging information
- trying to persuade each other
- making concessions and reaching agreement[14]

Generally, people in Western cultures take a relatively "transactional" approach to negotiation, focusing mainly on the last two stages. Many other cultures focus on creating a background relationship that will make agreement more likely, and emphasize the social side of the situation over the task side. The case of Bill Miller in Mexico is an example of people from two cultures not being able to negotiate with each other because each was stuck in a different part of the process. Culturally intelligent Americans learn to be sociable and patient in negotiation, and culturally intelligent Asians and Latinos learn to get to the point a more quickly.

Styles of persuasion may also differ. In political and business negotiating in Western societies, rational argument is favored, whereas in some other countries appeals to emotion or ideology may be used. Again, Western negotiators, having individualist values, are relatively competitive in their negotiating style, whereas Asians are likely to be more polite, more obscure, and more restrained. One researcher has used the metaphors of "sports" and "household" to explain the different approaches of American and Japanese negotiators. The sports metaphor of the individualist Americans suggests that they are task-oriented, accept conflict as normal, and try to conduct an orderly process with rules of procedure within which they have the chance to excel and win. The household metaphor of the more collectivist Japanese, in contrast, is focused on their relationships, their desire to avoid overt conflict and save face, and the fact that they gain satisfaction from the performance of their role rather than from winning.[15]

Another key cultural variable is power distance (see chapter 2), the extent to which people expect to see power and authority invoked to solve problems. The arbitration model of negotiation supposes that whenever there are differences of interest to be negotiated, there should be a higher-level authority figure who can resolve any problem by making a decision that is imposed on all parties. This is often observed in Japan. Another model is the bureaucratic one, which attempts to reduce the need for negotiation by specifying in advance rules and procedures suitable for solving disagreements. This model is often observed in Germany.

Again, there are differences in the details of negotiating:

for example, the level at which initial offers are made and the willingness of the negotiator to make concessions. An American negotiator might be put off by a Chinese, Arab, or Russian counterpart because these groups seem to start off with extreme positions. Russians are also reluctant to make concessions, seeing this as a sign of weakness, whereas other groups such as North Americans and Arabs will make concessions and respond to others' concessions. To complicate matters further, negotiators alter their behavior when they are negotiating with people from different countries. Finally, of course, the generalizations made above about different cultural groups' negotiating styles are subject to substantial individual differences.

In cross-cultural negotiation, it may be possible to use combinations of these different methods, but doing so requires all parties to step temporarily outside their normal conventions.

Principles for Cross-Cultural Communication and Negotiation

While plenty of information is available on cross-cultural communication and negotiation, from both everyday observation and systematic research, it is difficult to spell out hard-and-fast rules for communicating and negotiating. However, here are some broad principles.

- *Gain the knowledge to anticipate differences.* Learn what you can of the codes and conventions of groups that you plan to deal with. Be aware of all the various areas of difference in communication we have noted in this chapter—for example, verbal versus nonverbal, contextual versus noncontextual, different negotiating styles. Learn the prevailing cultural values of the country—for example, individualist versus collectivist—and think about how these may influence the process of your contacts.

- *Practice mindfulness.* Pay attention to the *context* and the *conventions* of communication. There is a tendency to focus on the code and content of messages, but you can acquire additional information by attending to *how* messages are delivered. Additionally, question attributions. In chapter 3 we discussed the process in which we go behind surface behavior of others to attribute motivation and meaning. As we have seen, the meaning we usually attribute is based on a familiar understanding of our own behavior and that of our cultural group. Practicing mindfulness helps us to see new possibilities for the meaning in the behavior of other cultural groups.

- *Develop cross-cultural skills.* How much should you adapt your behavior to accommodate the codes, conventions, and style of another culture? You and the other party have potentially conflicting goals, so this situation is challenging. Should you try to imitate them or just be yourself? Some adaptation seems to improve relationships by making the other party more comfortable, but too much adaptation can cause suspicion and distrust. Finding the optimal point of adaptation is more art than science. However, by improving your cultural intelligence, you can gain a broad repertoire of adaptive skills and the knowledge of when they are appropriate.

Summary

Communication is fundamental to all social interactions and relationships. Cross-cultural communication presents many possible barriers to shared understanding because individuals from different cultures don't share a common background, codes, or conventions. While language skills are important, cross-cultural communication involves much more than language differences. Culturally based codes and conventions of language also involve nonverbal signals and communication styles. Negotiation is a special communication situation in which the parties have potentially conflicting goals. While all negotiations follow a similar process, the emphasis placed on each stage varies considerably across cultures. The challenging nature of negotiations makes high cultural intelligence a prerequisite for knowing when, how, and how much to adapt one's behavior to achieve the most successful outcome.

CHAPTER 6

Motivating and Leading across Cultures

CLASS CONDUCT

Kenichi Tokuzawa, a Japanese man of twenty-four, was a university student of languages and was fluent in a number of Western languages, including English. He was also a skilled teacher, because, prior to his university study, he had trained as a schoolteacher and had taught for two years in a Japanese primary school. Kenichi had been acclaimed as an outstanding young teacher and put his success down to his clear structuring of class objectives and syllabi, his meticulous pre-class preparation, his articulate use of language, and his ability to make topics interesting for his students. The results were impressive: when Kenichi taught, every student paid close attention.

In his final year of language study, Kenichi, one of the best students in his group, won an international scholarship enabling him to spend a semester studying at a well-known university in New England. It was a most attractive opportunity, and, to top it off, it included the opportunity to teach, part-time and on salary, at a local high school, where he would conduct daily classes in conversational Japanese with a tenth-grade class of American students.

Kenichi was excited at the opportunity to combine his teaching background with his knowledge of both Japanese and English. He realized it would be a challenge to teach students from another culture who were much older than those he had taught before, but he reasoned that his thorough preparation and proven teaching techniques could transcend cultural boundaries. He had heard that American students take a more relaxed approach to their study and expect to participate more in class than do Japanese, but as a young Japanese well educated in U.S. culture, he thought he would be able to get on the same wavelength as American teenagers. As for class participation, that was essential in any form of language teaching, as students need to practice aloud the pronunciation of the new words they are learning.

On his first day in his new class, Kenichi, immaculately dressed, walked to the front of the classroom, bowed, smiled, and said, in excellent English, "Good morning. I am Mr. Tokuzawa. I am here to teach you Japanese." A few of the girls tittered, and several of the boys went on talking among themselves as if he had not spoken. A little rattled, Kenichi tapped the desk loudly with his pen. "Please listen to me," he said, more loudly, and repeated his greeting. This time there was more attention, but also further suppressed giggles. A youth at the back of the class, lounging in his chair, rolled his eyes toward the ceiling.

Kenichi realized there was a real possibility of a challenge to his authority, and he decided to impose it. Briskly, he asked a student to distribute his meticulously prepared course notes. Clearly and methodically, he explained the syllabus and grading system for the course. He asked if there were any questions. There were none. Rather than being eager to participate, the students seemed bored, listless. It was the same when he started teaching. He taught well, clearly, following exactly the carefully prepared schedule he had devised weeks before. He asked the students to repeat his words back and to translate, and a few did so. But it seemed that they did so unwillingly, as if they were answering his questions only to break the silence. The atmosphere at the front of the class was leaden. At the back of the class the students were restless. The boy who had rolled his eyes put his head down on his desk and appeared to go to sleep.

Dismissing the students at the end of the class, Kenichi overheard a girl remark to her friend as they exited, "Is that guy uptight! He ought to chill out." "Chill out"? He wasn't sure he knew the expression. But he did realize that his first class had been a major step backward. Whatever the reason, the class was just not in a mood to listen, to learn, to be led by him. Why? Were they just not interested in the subject? Were these simply the norms of the school, or the United States, in all classes? Or was there something he himself had simply got wrong?

In this case, the problem Kenichi faces is one of *leadership*. Leadership has been defined as "the ability to influence other people to strive willingly to reach common goals."[1] Kenichi is not just the teacher of the class, he is its leader. It is his job to get the class interested in the common goal of learning Japanese and influence them to "strive willingly" toward the goal.

Why has he not succeeded? While we do not know enough about the case to say for sure, it seems most likely that his style of leadership was too Japanese to achieve a good fit with the culture and expectations of his American students. Japanese have a higher level of power distance (see chapter 2) than Americans; that is, they expect and accept that a leader will exercise authority as a right. Japanese show more respect to leaders because of their positions, whereas in the United States leaders have to earn respect through their actions. In Japan, respect is shown partly by *not* participating, that is, by respecting what the leader says and does and waiting until the leader asks you to make a contribution before speaking. Japanese schoolchildren are therefore much more respectful of their teachers than Americans are and much more ready to pay attention and accept the teacher's instruction without question. The Americans in Kenichi's class might have responded better if he had been less formal and had found out more about them—by being mindful—before launching into his own agenda. Kenichi will have his work cut out for him if he is to get his students to be receptive. Can Kenichi motivate this class? Is he a leader?

Motivation across Cultures

In order for a person to lead, he or she must be able to understand the basic motivation of those being led—their willingness to exert effort toward a goal. Patterns of motivation vary both between individuals and across cultures. For example, achievement motivation (striving for individual success) is likely to be higher in individualist cultures, and affiliation motivation (seeking to develop good interpersonal relationships) may be higher in a collectivist culture, but in both cases there may be individuals who are exceptions. And there is some evidence that culturally based levels of achievement motivation contribute to the level of entrepreneurial activity in a society.

In organizations and other collective settings, an important aspect of motivation is the attitude of individuals to the allocation of rewards. Here, the issue of equity (fair distribution of rewards) versus equality (equal distribution of rewards) is important. The culture variable power distance (see chapter 2) tends to be related to preference for equity (which leads to more unequal rewards) over equality. Collectivist societies prefer more equally distributed rewards for in-group members, whereas individualist societies believe that individual performance should be rewarded with benefits related to the level of performance of the individual.

The relationship of all this to leadership is that it is the leader's task to determine the key motives of followers and find ways to provide incentives relating these motives to performance in the form of a rewards system appropriate to the cultural and individual characteristics of the situation. This task makes leaders such as Kenichi Tokuzawa motivational diagnosticians of their situation. What are the underlying motives of the followers? How can these be mobilized? How can effective action be rewarded? These are key leadership questions.

Popular Ideas of Leadership

There is much public confusion about leadership. Many people believe in the "Great Man" theory of leadership and have an individual in mind who personifies leadership to them—such as Gandhi, John F. Kennedy, Joan of Arc, or Sun Tzu. We think of such people as having a high-level gift of leadership as a result of which they can lead effectively regardless of situation, task, or culture. However, several questions arise, the answers to which can help us to become more culturally intelligent leaders.

- What made these people leaders and other people not?
- Would these people have been great leaders at another time, in another place, or indeed in another culture?
- Would these people have been great leaders with different followers, particularly followers who were culturally different from them?

A parallel to the Great Man theory is the "One Best Way" theory. Many people believe that there is a set of definable practices, almost a magic formula, that will bring inevitable success in leadership regardless of situation.

Leadership would certainly be easier to arrange if either theory were true. Unfortunately both theories are just plain wrong.[2] Many people—both men and women—may exercise effective leadership in different situations and cultures, and those effective in one situation will not necessarily be so in another. Likewise, effective leaders influence their followers in different ways. A leader may capture the loyalty of some followers while being rejected and ridiculed by others. A style that works perfectly in one situation (such as with construction workers in Dubai) may fall flat in another (such as with software engineers in Silicon Valley).

Even without taking the cultural dimension into account,

leaders need to display the mindfulness and adaptability skills discussed in chapter 3 just to understand the special features of the situation and vary their leadership to fit the amount of power at their disposal, the characteristics of their followers, and the tasks to be accomplished. Including cultural intelligence in leadership is a major challenge. Yet as more and more leaders find themselves, as Kenichi Tokuzawa did, dealing with followers who are culturally different from themselves (and often culturally different from each other) in settings where different traditions and expectations for leadership exist, it is vital for any leader or prospective leader to develop a culturally intelligent approach.

Leadership Styles

Our understanding of culturally intelligent leadership begins with a look at leadership styles—a concept based on research conducted in the United States that has been assumed to be valid and has sometimes been applied around the world. These studies attempted to relate organizational performance—as indicated by measures such as productivity, quality, and staff morale—to different styles of leadership behavior. Two dimensions of leadership style that have shown up consistently are *concern for tasks* (getting things done, achieving organizational goals) and *concern for relationships* (getting along well with people, involving them so that they participate in decision making). Research indicates conclusively and unsurprisingly that relationship-oriented leaders tend to have more satisfied subordinates and that this is true across a range of different cultures.[3]

However, most organizations are at least as interested in employees' performance as in their satisfaction, and the evidence on whether leadership style is related to performance is more complex. Task-oriented leadership, for example, can be demonstrated in different ways—for example, by meticulous goal-directed planning or by autocratic command. Moreover, people from different cultures react to task-oriented leadership in different and often unpredictable ways. There are also numerous other factors, such as the structure of the task, the power of the leader, and the behavior of subordinates—who, of course, are frequently trying to influence the leader just as he or she is trying to influence them—so that many possible propositions about leadership must be hedged with the proviso "it depends." In short, researchers are still a long way short of finding the "one best way" of leadership that is applicable across all cultures. In the next section we consider examples of leadership around the world. By looking at such examples, we can begin to understand the enormous complexity and subtlety of the cultural forces affecting leadership.

Leadership around the World

THE ARAB WORLD

Leadership in Arab societies is a fascinating example of how history and culture can influence the traditions, practices, and expectations of leadership. Islamic religion and tribal traditions have always been strong and remain so, but Arabic countries are now touched by Western culture. Islam tends to make leadership a prerogative of males. Tribal traditions oblige leaders to behave like fathers, protecting and nurturing followers such as employees as they would their children and taking responsibility for the whole enterprise. Overlaying this system is the notion of bureaucracy, historically introduced by the Ottoman Empire and continued by Europeans in the twentieth century as a way of keeping control of their businesses and other institutions.

The resultant leadership style has been termed "sheikhocracy."[4] It contains strong elements of personal autocracy and conformity to rules and regulations based on respect for those who made the rules rather than for the rules' rationality. Rules thus have symbolic importance but will not be implemented if they go against autocratic-tribal traditions: for example, the bureaucracy may specify procedures for appointment on merit, but in the event these rules are likely to be ignored. Instead a leader will make appointments based on family relationships and friendships.

JAPAN

In Japan, one of the key factors that influence leadership is the cultural value of *amae*. *Amae* (somewhat loosely translated) means indulgent love, the kind that parents have for their children. In some societies, dependence on parents is socialized out of children at an early age, and they are taught to be independent and to stand on their own two feet. In Japan, all relationships, including manager-subordinate relationships, are affected by *amae*. It is therefore not surprising to find that Japanese managers take a deep interest in employees' personal lives. Subordinates often ask superiors for advice on all sorts of things, including personal matters such as who would make a good spouse.

The existence of *amae* in Japanese relationships also gives rise to other cultural norms that influence leader behavior. Leader behavior in Japan is embedded in a network of reciprocal obligations (*on* and *giri*). *On* is a debt or obligation, and *giri* is the moral obligation to repay the debt. Thus, every action creates both a debt and an obligation to repay. A leader who neglects the obligation to reciprocate will lose the trust and support of followers. A Japanese leader's effectiveness is thus based, more than anything else, on the ability to understand and attract followers.[5]

THE OVERSEAS CHINESE

Ethnic Chinese living outside mainland China have a leadership style that reflects their modern organizations but is firmly entrenched in Chinese culture and tradition. In Chinese culture a leader's legitimacy is based on loyalty to the patriarch. Similarly, the word of the founder or CEO of modern Chinese organizations is law, and his authority resembles that of a head of the household more than that of a head of a business. All key people in the organization are related to the founder, and to each other, by blood or marriage. This authority structure allows the overseas Chinese to run their modern corporation as a family business. Mutual trust among family members—to base decisions on what is best for the clan—underlies all leader-follower relationships.[6]

FRANCE

Leadership in France is heavily influenced by the strong societal emphasis on hierarchy. At the top of French organizations is the CEO, who will have attended the "right" university, one of the Grandes Écoles. The style of these top managers is often paternalistic and charismatic in the style of the great field marshals of France.[7] Between the top managers and the workers is a large group of middle managers or *cadres,* who deal with a plethora of rules and regulations. While seeming bewilderingly inefficient to the outsider, these organizations operate very reliably.

RUSSIA

The image of Russian leaders as powerful autocrats is based on the country's long history of centralized authority and responsibility.[8] In medieval Russia, village elders were entrusted to represent the common will of the people, and suggestions and criticisms were never attributable to any one individual. It was the elders' task to sort through the comments, and once they made their decisions, these went unchallenged and the elders bore full responsibility for the welfare of the group. Later, under state socialism, these same traditional attitudes toward power and responsibility were evident in communist organizations. Although advised by workers councils, the heads of these enterprises wielded all the power and also bore all the responsibility.

This centralization of power resulted in a top-heavy bureaucracy that some suggest was the fatal flaw in the socialist system. When things went wrong, as they often did, no one would take action without authorization from a superior. As Russian firms try to find their way in their new free-market environment, managers now struggle to push responsibility down the hierarchy and to delegate routine tasks. Consider the following case:

MANAGEMENT BY OBJECTIVES IN RUSSIA

Dahl Ekelund, a Norwegian who was newly appointed executive director of the Russian subsidiary of Motor Corporation, was conducting a seminar with his seventeen subordinate managers to introduce the concept of Management by Objectives (MBO).[9] Dahl had recently been appointed by the board of directors in the hope that his extensive track record as a leader in various European engineering enterprises would enable him to release some of the potential in a workforce that was well-qualified, talented, and experienced but knew little about market-based enterprise or modern management.

Dahl was amazed by the undisguised hostility directed not only at what he was saying but also at himself as the executive director. When he started to discuss the need for all employees to set their own written objectives, his subordinates actively came out against the proposal with comments such as: "We have lived without this kind of thing for five years and have made great strides. And we are still thriving. We don't need a new bureaucracy."

Dahl explained how MBO works and how it provides new opportunities for staff involvement and participation at all levels. This brought the retort that he was not the first to try to implement Western managerial methods in the company—nobody had succeeded, and those who had tried were now working somewhere else.

Clearly irritated, Dahl answered brusquely, "Anybody working around me is going to be using these modern methods."

After this comment, you could have heard a pin drop.

In conclusion, Dahl said that he expected a written outline of the next year's goals from each of his subordinates within two weeks. He also asked them to get the same information from their own subordinates within three weeks.

As he left the room, Dahl overheard the following comments:

"Well, now, Petrovich, you'll be establishing goals rather than working."

"Not in my lifetime, let him do it himself."

"But, what about the bonus? Didn't you hear, only those who reach the goals get the bonus."

"Yeah, we'll see."[10]

In the case above, the leadership expectations of the Russian subordinates are shaped by both Russian culture and years of living and working in organizations still influenced by the remnants of state socialism. These Russian middle managers demonstrate an expectation for autocratic leadership and have great difficulty accepting, or trusting, their own participation or that of their subordinates in setting goals. Their reluctance is exacerbated by a healthy skepticism about the extent to which their superiors are concerned with, or capable of, controlling their futures, because under state socialism each autocratic boss was someone else's puppet. These beliefs persist long after the demise of the socialist policies that created them.

In seeking to help the company move into a more market-oriented future, a higher-CQ Dahl Ekelund might have applied cultural intelligence by

- avoiding the *Be Like Me* approach to management that he had learned based on his cultural background in Western Europe (*knowledge*)

- taking more time to learn in detail some of the special characteristics of the new culture that he was entering (*knowledge*)

- spending time observing and talking to his new subordinates for a few weeks after arrival, trying to understand their collective and individual areas of comfort and discomfort before trying to institute change (*mindfulness*)

- trying to understand from the Russian perspective *why* they might be acting the way they were (*mindfulness*)

- listening to what his staff were saying (and being aware of what they were not saying) rather than becoming irritated and walking out of the meeting (*mindfulness and adaptive behavior*)
- introducing a less ambitious form of MBO, for example, one in which leaders set goals for their subordinates at first and then made a more gradual move toward participative methods (*adaptive behavior*)

These examples from Arab countries, China, Japan, France, and Russia show the complexity of the forces affecting leadership. Note the importance of historical factors, tradition rather than reason, and the acceptance, under the right circumstances, of apparently autocratic leadership. Individuals with high cultural intelligence are mindfully attentive to such factors and work hard to develop even deeper knowledge. An international manager known to one of the authors, whose job took him into leadership roles all around the globe, would voraciously read books on the history and customs of the countries he was due to visit in order to acquire background knowledge and sensitivity to the local situation.

Culture and Expectations of Followers

As suggested above, another aspect of culturally intelligent leadership involves focusing not on the leader but on the followers. In some ways the idea of leadership is an invention of those who want to be in charge or who believe that their traditional or hierarchical positions entitle them to be in charge. But in a sense, everyone is in charge; everyone has the potential to exercise leadership. We have defined leadership in terms of influence, and influence may be exercised by anyone, from the highest to the lowest member of an organization. Therefore, in understanding how leadership works across cultures, we need to look at all participants—how they might understand a situation, whether they might expect a leader to decide for them what they should do, or whether and how they might seek to exercise influence in their own right. Thus, even low-level members of an organization who are working within their own culture may be major assets in terms of offering cultural understanding in a leadership process.

The designated leader needs to think not just about how he or she might exercise influence but about how that influence might interact with the influence exercised by others to bring about a good result. For example, Dahl Ekelund, if he is smart, can set goals for his subordinates exactly as they want him to, yet still use the formal and informal processes that are part of their culture to find out their views and consider them before determining the goals.

To begin to understand the leadership expectations of different cultural groups, let us recap the key values dimensions outlined in chapter 2.

- In *individualist* cultures, people are concerned about themselves, prefer activities to be conducted privately, and expect decisions to be made by the individual according to his or her judgment and the anticipated rewards.

- In *collectivist* cultures, people view themselves as members of groups and collectives, prefer group activities, and expect decisions to be made on a consensual or consultative basis, where the effects of the decision on everyone are taken into account.

Two very different styles of leadership would be expected in the two types of cultures. Western countries tend to be individualist, so both leaders and followers will attempt to involve themselves in influence processes to maximize their individual influence and gain for themselves a good result. Higher management frequently tries to utilize individualism to advantage by offering the leader a high individual reward for the accomplishments of the group or by holding the individual leader accountable for the performance of the group as a whole. Collectivist societies can rely more on the leader to involve the group, because that will be the shared expectation of both leader and group members.

Other cultural forces influence expectations of leaders in similar ways. Some cultures value formality, and a leader will be expected to honor appropriate ceremonies and observances. In cultures where punctuality is important, there will be pressure on leaders to turn up on time. In future-oriented societies, a leader will be expected to focus on long-term strategy and to express that focus in his or her words. Because of the special status of the position, the leader is often the most led member of the group—led, that is, by the cultural milieu in which he or she exercises leadership.

In many societies, historical and cultural forces—such as high power distance, Confucianism, and feudalism—the practice and expectation of a style of leadership has developed that can best be described as *paternalistic*.[11] Paternalism involves creating a family atmosphere at work, having close relationships with followers to the extent of getting involved in their non–work lives, and expecting both deference and loyalty. Paternalism often generates positive employee attitudes, and some Western organizations have been tempted to utilize paternalism as a means of securing a contented, compliant workforce. In the wrong cultural milieu, though, such efforts can backfire.[12]

Leading in Multinational Organizations

Leading any organization or group with a culturally diverse workforce requires cultural intelligence. But in the case of large multinational organizations with subsidiaries in many different countries, the problem is increased. Typically there are organizational requirements for central control and uniformity in such matters as finance and operations, just to ensure that the organization remains stable and subsidiaries work toward a common goal. But when such organizations attempt to manage their own diverse communities of people in a uniform manner, major problems emerge, as the following case shows.

THE COMMON BOND

Jenny Gendall is a secretary employed by the New Zealand office of Technica, a U.S.-based multinational organization providing IT hardware and support. Technica has offices in over seventy countries around the world.[13] In an attempt to respond to the cultural diversity engendered by its multinational workforce, Technica has implemented many new policies and procedures in this area, including a nondiscrimination policy for employment procedures. This policy states that the company will

> hire, train, promote and pay individuals based on their job-related qualifications, ability and performance without regard to color, race, ethnic, or national origin, sex, family status, religious or ethical belief, age, disability, political opinion, employment status, sexual orientation, presence in body of organisms capable of causing illness, association or lack of association with an employee organization.

More recently, Technica's head office in the United States has developed a set of values designed to provide a framework which all Technica employees, in every country, will use in their day-to-day actions. The values are to reflect Technica's "critical success factors" to differentiate the company from its competitors and to make it a better place to work by offering shared values to all employees. The statement of values is known as Our Common Bond, and one value, focusing the issues of diversity referred to above, is respect for the individual: "We treat each other with respect and dignity, valuing individual and cultural differences. We communicate frequently and with candor, listening to each other regardless of level or position."

An action plan for implementing Our Common Bond has been disseminated internationally from the head office. Each subsidiary, including New Zealand, has received detailed directives, manuals, training programs, videos, and visits by international facilitators to ensure conformity. To Jenny Gendall, who considers that the New

Zealand office has always been a pretty good place to work in terms of respect, valuing equity, and all the rest of it, it seems like a lot of fuss about nothing.

Indeed, some Technica New Zealand employees are beginning to question the suitability and compatibility of the values, the language used, and the method of implementation. The values are being imposed without discussion and are in what Jenny and some of her colleagues consider to be "American language" and are inappropriate within New Zealand.

According to Jenny, "The Common Bond stuff really is just about day-to-day courtesy. It doesn't need to be spelled out; we shouldn't need to be told. I'm not sure why it was forced on the entire company; maybe it's a strategy to get rid of some of a few people who won't change. I hate that airy-fairy, warm-fuzzy stuff. I just want to get on with the job. We're free and easy over here, and the Common Bond just doesn't suit our Kiwi style. And anyway we're all different. The Common Bond says we need to 'listen to each other regardless level or position,' but I can tell you some of our Maori and Pacific Island employees still expect to show, and be shown, proper respect for status."

In this case, Technica's head office hopes to lead the establishment of a corporate culture that will encompass all of the international subsidiaries. But its universal set of values cannot easily be translated across cultural boundaries—even between apparently similar cultures like the United States and New Zealand—as they have the potential to act as a touchstone for the recognition of contradiction and cultural conflict. Although Technica is genuinely international and culturally diverse, there is still a definite "home" culture emanating from the U.S. head office; and, notwithstanding its talk of embracing diversity, in its global leadership Technica is not truly "walking the walk." Rather, subsidiaries are asked to adopt U.S.-developed values and procedures that appear to have little regard to their suitability for other cultures. The effect, at least in New Zealand, is that instead of embracing diversity, employees tend to criticize, ignore, and subvert the changes.

"Managing diversity" is a positive goal for multinational corporations, but the mechanisms for achieving it need to be locally specific and probably locally devised. The notion of "think globally and act locally" is a useful tenet for managing diversity in international organizations.

Also important in this case is the question of "who is leader"? It has long been known that there is a difference between formal leadership (in which the leader is formally appointed and has an appropriate job title) and informal leadership (in which someone has leadership status because of the respect of others). Informal leaders arise because their ideas or behavior are well received by others and because they practice good communication skills in putting their ideas across. Thus, in the case above, informal leaders in New Zealand subvert the leadership of corporate bosses in the United States. Ideally, the formal and informal leaders are the same person, but often in a cross-cultural situation a formal leader from another culture may be poorly accepted because of cultural differences—particularly differences in expected methods of leadership—and there may be an informal leader from the home culture representing the ideas of the rank and file and exercising countervailing influence. This can make it important for formal leaders either to exercise a leadership style that fits in with local expectations or to be able to work with the informal leader.

Cultural differences in expectations of leadership also affect the perception of who is thought of as a leader. Different cultures have different prototypes of what a leader should be like. A leader who is able to meet followers' expectations of a good leader can develop better trust and relationships with the group.

Followership

Modern theories of leadership recognize that if we take seriously the definition of leadership—the ability to influence other people to strive willingly to reach common goals— it is evident that anyone in a group, and not just the formal boss, has the potential to be a leader. In most groups, leadership is shared to some extent. Further, the exercise of leadership implies a duty of followers to follow. Therefore, in multicultural groups and organizations, the acquisition of cultural intelligence is of advantage to the apparent follower as well as the leader. Being able to "read" one's formal leader and colleagues taking into account their national culture is an advantage in any situation. Cultural intelligence is for everyone, not just top leaders!

The Common Thread: Charismatic or Transformational Leadership

An idea that has dominated thinking about leadership in recent decades is transformational leadership, which influences people to transcend their own immediate interests and objectives and to work hard to achieve not just desired performance but performance beyond expectations.[14] To do this, the leader has to present not just an immediate reward for behavior but also a compelling vision of the future. The leader must aim not just to motivate members but also to inspire them, must demonstrate or model the behavior desired from followers, must stimulate and challenge followers, and must show individual consideration to each follower—tasks that are facilitated if the leader has the cultural knowledge and mindfulness characteristic of high CQ.

Perhaps the easiest way to understand transformational leadership is to return to the type of well-known leader such as Winston Churchill, John F. Kennedy, and Martin Luther King Jr. However, Eastern leaders such as the Indian political and spiritual leader Mohandas Gandhi also meet the criteria for transformational leadership, as does the great South African leader Nelson Mandela, even though they may have practiced it in a very different and much lower-key way, and one that was in tune with the expectations and cultural values of their followers. Note the cultural variety of these exemplars. A leader with high cultural intelligence will be able to provide a vision, engage others' motivation, and model behavior in ways consistent with the culture and values of followers.

Indeed, there is research that supports the effectiveness of transformational leadership across a range of different countries.[15] Yet people from different countries have different ways of expecting leaders to act, even within a shared overall definition of transformational leadership, and there may be countries, such as Japan, where for a variety of cultural reasons its effectiveness is limited. In any case, it may be that the practice of transformational leadership requires special personal characteristics that may not be available in every leader. It is even more important to get the basics right in terms of understanding how to fit concern for task and concern for people within the specifics of the cultural setting.

Culturally Intelligent Leadership

Making sense of leadership is difficult enough, even without the complication of cultural differences. While there is no universally effective prescription for leading culturally diverse followers, there are some things we can say for certain that culturally intelligent leaders know and do.

- Leadership is largely in the minds of followers. If followers perceive a person as a leader, he or she will gain the power, authority, and respect afforded a leader.

- Some characteristics that followers look for in a leader are (a) a vision for the group or organization, (b) the ability to clearly communicate this vision to others, and (c) skill in organizing followers toward that vision. However, the behavior that indicates these characteristics is different in different cultures.

- The leadership dimensions of task orientation and relationship orientation exist in every culture. Again, however, the behaviors that indicate a task orientation rather than a relationship orientation are specific to different cultures.

- Some followers need more leading along each of these dimensions than others. Factors such as organizational norms and the education levels of followers can act as substitutes for leadership. For example, a group of research scientists typically needs vary little in the way of task orientation from their leader. They already know what to do.

- Finally, trying to mimic the behavior of a leader belonging to the followers' culture can often lead to unintended consequences. Some adoption of these behaviors will gain a leader acceptance by followers, but too much can be interpreted as insincere or even offensive.[16]

In summary, if you want to be a culturally intelligent leader, you will need to use knowledge and mindfulness to develop a repertoire of behaviors that can be adapted to each specific situation. Doing so involves knowledge of the likely expectations of followers in different cultures based on generalizations from cultural values like individualism and collectivism. Through mindful observation, you will refine these expectations over time. However, you will also need knowledge of your own preferred style of leadership. What balance of task and relationship orientation feels normal to you? Will you have to work harder at being a relational leader if the situation calls for it?

You will also need knowledge of what organizational norms exist in your situation. Trying to be a participative boss in a culture that does not value participation can be counterproductive. Here, mindfulness also means paying attention to follower reactions to particular leadership behaviors and adjusting as necessary.

In cross-cultural situations, it is probably best not to model your leader behavior after a leader in the follower culture. In addition to looking silly trying to behave like Sun Tzu (if you are not Chinese), you may find that follower expectations of indigenous leaders may be very different from their expectations of you. Also, in multicultural groups followers can have very different expectations. Therefore, a better role model is a leader like you (e.g., someone from your own culture) who has been particularly effective with these followers.

That is, the needs of followers are extremely important in determining an individual's perceptions of leadership. In the end, however, a culturally intelligent leader is able to find a leadership style that strikes a balance between his or her preferred (normal) style, the expectations of followers, and the demands of the situation. This balance is always likely to be imperfect, a work in progress. As with surfing or skiing or riding a bike, finding this balance is initially very difficult but becomes easier and feels more natural over time.

Summary

In this chapter we introduced the problem of practicing culturally intelligent leadership. Influencing others toward goals is difficult in itself. However, when the dynamics of cross-cultural interactions are added, the challenge is even greater. Our understanding of leadership is greatly influenced by individuals we envision as great leaders, who share a similar ability to communicate a vision and to organize followers. In addition, the idea that leaders can exhibit a task or relationship leadership style has a universal appeal. However, the variety of behaviors that leaders around the world exhibit raises questions about any universal approach to leadership. This chapter suggests that understanding the expectations that followers have of their leaders is a key element in a culturally intelligent approach to leadership. This, plus an individual's preferred style and the constraints imposed by the situation, provide the three dimensions among which the culturally intelligent leader must find balance. While initially difficult to achieve, this equilibrium becomes easier with each iteration of the knowledge, mindfulness, and behavioral skills process of cultural intelligence.

Working with Multicultural
Groups and Teams

PARTICIPATE, AND THAT'S AN ORDER!

Harry is the leader of an advertising agency account team. The team's task is to develop advertising campaigns for a manufacturing company's range of power lawnmowers. The four members of the team are all from different cultural backgrounds. And they seem to be at odds with each other.

Harry, an American, has strong ideas about what the campaign should be like; he talks about it a lot and tries to persuade his three colleagues. But despite his strong views, Harry recognizes the value of diversity, of different ideas. He makes it clear to his colleagues that he *welcomes* alternative ideas. He would be delighted if someone was to come up with a campaign idea that was better than his. Harry says frequently, "Two heads are better than one, and four heads are better than two." His three team members eye each other cautiously.

So far the only person who has responded to Harry's invitation is Ingrid, a recent immigrant from Germany. Ingrid has ideas about the lawnmower campaign that are not only different from Harry's but also completely opposite. Furthermore, she has had twenty years' experience in the industry back in Germany and believes she has forgotten more about advertising than Harry ever learned. She is not about to back down on her ideas. She too talks, frequently and forcefully, about the new campaign. Harry doesn't agree with her and argues back, loudly. But after all he did say he values alternatives.

The other two members of the team keep a low profile. José, who is of Latin American background, can't stand Ingrid. How *dare* she talk to the boss like that! Has she no respect for authority? It's not so much that José doesn't agree with Ingrid's ideas—in fact secretly he thinks they are quite good; it's the rude and aggressive way she presents them and her contemptuous way of treating Harry as if she were equal to him, if not higher, that he objects to. José would rather cut his arm off than encourage Ingrid by supporting her ideas. So he sides quietly with Harry and wishes Ingrid would go away.

Ming is a Taiwanese with a demure exterior, and although she is an expert in this type of campaign, she too keeps quiet. Harry says he wants her opinions and ideas, but she doesn't think he means it. If he does, why does he argue so aggressively with Ingrid? If you really want to hear what other people think, Ming believes, you should behave as if you respect them. Listening to Harry and Ingrid makes Ming sad. These people are talented but completely ego-centric. Ming believes good decisions are made through patient reflection, the respectful exchange of ideas, and the protection of the harmony of the group that will, after all, have to work together to implement the final decision. She wishes she knew how to implement this method with Harry and Ingrid. In the meantime, she puts forward her views when Harry asks her, but she speaks so timidly that Harry wonders if Ming herself believes what she is saying.

The differences in the group can be explained largely by the cultural variation that we introduced in chapter 2. Westerners such as Harry and Ingrid tend to be high on individualism and autonomy and moderate or low on power distance and hierarchy. This means that they will expect to put forward their own views strongly in a group situation. Furthermore, they have been brought up and educated to be articulate and persuasive in the way they talk. They tend to believe in a kind of creative conflict in which ideas are pitted against each other until the best one wins. Maybe if Harry and Ingrid stick to it long enough, one will eventually persuade the other. But unless they are able to separate the ideas from the person presenting them, the growing rivalry between the two may make it difficult for either to admit that the other is right.

As for the others, it appears that José has such a high level of power distance—and the associated expectation that decisions should be made by those in authority—that he is unable to accept Ingrid's form of intervention. And Ming appears to be a collectivist who is a little lost in an individualists' world: she expects modest harmonious discussions in which the goals of the group as a whole take precedence over individuals' egos. In a group where Ingrid expects the right to challenge, José expects the imposition of authority, and Ming expects a long, courteous decision process without conflict, it seems unlikely that a creative discussion will ensue.

Each member of the team explicitly adopts both the behavior and the norms implicit in his or her cultural background. Each has brought to this new group his or her own culturally based ideas for how groups should function. There is little evidence of mindfulness in the way they interact with one another. In both action and in observation, they stick to culturally predetermined scripts.

Yet each of them has much to offer. Each has technical expertise vital to the group's task. Harry and Ingrid are full of ideas and articulate in presenting them. Ming has ideals of team harmony and respect for listening, and José recognizes the ultimate need for decisiveness by the leader and acceptance of decisions; both have much to offer the group. In this case, as in so many cases, diversity of cultural background is not just a problem to be solved; it is an opportunity to be capitalized on. Despite the conflict in the group, its diversity adds huge potential if they could but see it and harness it.

The Challenge of Teams

In addition to the increasing cultural diversity of the work-force mentioned previously in this book, there is another, related pressure: an increasing emphasis, in the way business is organized, on *teams*. Because of the growing diversity of the workforce, such teams, even in one's home country, are becoming more and more multicultural. This shift presents a dual challenge: how to *contribute* to a multicultural team and how to *manage* a multicultural team.

Once people are organized into teams and expected to work collaboratively for the common good, it becomes impossible for the manager to try to handle multiculturalism by dealing with each employee individually according to his or her own cultural needs. He or she now has to manage not only a set of culturally different individuals but a *process* involving different cultural responses.

An important feature of how groups work is the difference between *task* and *process* activities.[1] Task activities are those that are directed toward accomplishing the goal the group is trying to achieve. For example, "This is my plan for the advertising campaign . . . "; "If we do it that way, we will run over budget"; "That's a good suggestion." Process activities are directed at examining and improving the ways in which the group goes about this task. For example, "Suppose we go around the group seeing what each person thinks before we start arguing about things"; "I think Jane has something to say, but no one is listening to her"; "We're running short of time, and we'd better have a vote now." Process activities need not be positive: "I'm irritated that even when I ask for your ideas you won't tell me what they are"; "I feel intimidated when you argue so loudly"; "In my country we show respect for other people."

Although it is right and proper that groups should spend most of their time dealing with the task at hand, failure to attend to process is a frequent cause of group dysfunction. Groups often become ineffective because their process is overly autocratic or torn apart by personal conflicts or indecisive, and they have no way of examining what they are doing and changing it. The problem is increased when the processes are complicated by cultural differences.

In the case above, the successful conclusion of the group task is a joint problem-solving objective. This depends on effective integration of ideas among all members of the group. However, the group's problems are culturally determined process problems. The participants all have different models in their heads of how the group process should work, but—due in part to the leader's preoccupation with the task and his assumption that the process will look after itself—they have no way of bringing these ideas to the surface and resolving the process issues.

Cultural intelligence provides a means of dealing with group development and process issues that are caused or exacerbated by cultural differences. However, cultural intelligence may also help solve the process problems associated with any group. High cultural intelligence enables the observing and understanding of the different actions and intentions of group members. It acknowledges the cultural diversity of the group and the legitimacy of each member and his or her cultural background. Understanding how members see their roles in the group is likely to improve the quality of its interpersonal interactions. Combining this awareness with an initial focus on getting group processes clear before proceeding to the detail of the task, the team described above could break its impasse and move on to a united achievement of its goal.

Applying all this to the case above, a culturally intelligent Harry who understood group processes would have recognized that his way of trying to lead the group was informed by his own cultural background and by the individualism and egalitarianism that were part of his makeup and that of his co-worker Ingrid. He might have given some thought to how he might modify his behavior in order to accommodate José and Ming's different characteristics. By attending mindfully to the others' reactions and doing some basic homework on the cultures they came from, he might have begun to understand Jose's deep-seated respect for authority and the fact that the quiet Ming had hidden depths. By modifying his own actions in a way that respected their difference from him, he might have gained a reciprocal response, such that Ingrid listened more and José and Ming became more forthcoming. By explicitly bringing up process issues in team meetings, he might have enabled a task orientation and a contribution to the group's task where all the team members were actively participating. Such a process would have not only improved task performance, it would have made the team more harmonious and its members more satisfied, and all of them would have improved their cultural intelligence.

Multicultural Teams Are Everywhere!

You don't have to go overseas to experience multicultural teams firsthand. You almost certainly don't even have to go outside your own organization. You probably don't have to go beyond your own immediate work group, sports club, or voluntary organization. Most of us have direct superiors, colleagues, subordinates, or friends whose cultural backgrounds are different from our own.

Some of these will be new immigrants, still struggling to adapt to the host culture. Others will be the children and grandchildren of immigrants, fluent in their new language and skilled in the practices and norms of the host culture but perhaps still influenced by the cultural norms and values that are inherent in their backgrounds: for example, a Muslim woman in a European country who no longer wears the *hijab* (a scarf that covers the head and neck) but still acts deferentially to her male colleagues and is unwilling to speak her mind freely;[2] or a courteous Chinese, unable fully to understand the boisterous mock aggression of his English colleagues to each other and why they smile when calling each other insulting names; or a naturally ebullient American depressed by the long silences of her Asian colleagues and trying desperately to create some sociability in such an earnest work environment. Workforces all around the world are becoming more culturally diverse, and the effect is felt at a local level.

This creates a challenge, beyond those already considered, for the development of cultural intelligence. The task of the manager, and indeed the members, of any work group becomes not just to practice cultural intelligence but also *to engender and encourage cultural intelligence in all members of the team* in their everyday interactions with each other and their overall work for the organization. Managing cultural differences in work groups is not just managing a set of one-to-one relationships between oneself and others from different cultures. It can often mean managing situations in which the cultural difference among those being managed is itself an issue, as in the case that opened this chapter.

Types of Work Groups

Groups are not all the same.[3] One group of workers may have relatively independent jobs but may be placed in the same workspace or have the same boss. We might call these groups *crews*. Another group of workers may collaborate closely with each other in a process in which the specialist knowledge of each member has to be closely integrated with that of the others. A good name for such groups is *teams*. A third group may be a temporary group expected to solve a specific problem or produce a report or design and then disband. This third type of group is often called a *task force*.

These differences are important because they involve different ways of working together and therefore put more or less pressure on the cultural aspect of group functioning. Knowing when cultural intelligence matters most can help us structure work groups effectively and understand why cultural differences have a big effect in some organizational groups and not in others. In crews, group functioning is often predetermined by set procedures and technology, which to some extent makes high levels of cultural intelligence unnecessary. Task forces such as the one in our case might benefit from higher cultural intelligence but may not need to build long-term intercultural relationships. Teams, however, require highly developed trusting long-term interrelationships between their members, and cultural intelligence, the management of intercultural differences, and the realization of cross-cultural potential are critical.

Group Process and Performance

In both face-to-face and virtual teams, group effectiveness is typically assessed by objective measures of group output such as production, quality, sales, and so on. However, group morale and cohesiveness are also important, as they tend to ensure that performance is maintained over time. In assessing groups, therefore, wise group leaders consider not just immediate performance but also the processes that the group uses to do its work, as well as the satisfaction and development of group members as a result of the experience. The cultural dimension makes the task of facilitating an effective group process more challenging.

Groups are more than just collections of individuals within an organization, and they form their own social processes. Watching an effective team perform can be very exciting; being a member of one, even better. Some teams can, through their own natural processes, spontaneously create a dynamic of performance or innovation that external influence simply could not prearrange. In particular, in response to the feel-good aspect of working on an intrinsically interesting problem with others who are different (but complementary) in their skills and outlooks, workers may release huge and hitherto unrealized energy or creativity or ideas. It is often exciting to feel the stimulus to thinking that we get from someone who is from a different background, who thinks and talks in a completely novel way. Different cultures increase the range of viewpoints and approaches available and are therefore a potential asset in many group situations. The trick is to create a process that encourages diverse team members and capitalizes on their differences to create this synergy.

On the other hand, groups can develop negative processes that undermine the potential of individual group members and reduce group effectiveness. Two commonly found such processes are known as groupthink and social loafing.

- In *groupthink* the group overemphasizes harmony and consensus by killing off dissent and creative alternatives.[4] A famous historical example was the *Challenger* disaster of 1986, where teams of officials at NASA and in the supplying company Morton Thiokol were under intense pressure to ensure that the attempt to send Challenger into space was successful and on time, and as a result of this groupthink, they would not listen to engineers who were telling them that a vital component was likely to fail in cold weather. In the event, the launch was authorized in cold conditions, the component failed a minute or two after takeoff, and the spacecraft exploded, killing all on board.

- In *social loafing* individuals reduce their efforts to complete group tasks in the belief that others in the group will compensate to get the job done.[5] In classic experiments on tug-of-war teams, for example, it was found that as more and more members were added to a team, the average exertion that members of the team applied to the rope decreased.[6] Anyone who has been involved in completing group projects will have noticed this phenomenon. There often seems to be at least one person who is not doing his or her part.

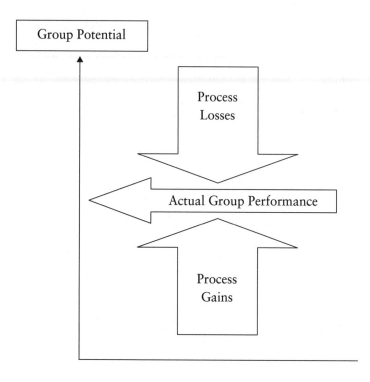

FIGURE 7.1.   Effect of process on group performance

Individualists, interestingly, are likely to take a stand against groupthink but are also more likely to take advantage of the group situation by social loafing. It is easy to see how cultural differences such as individualism-collectivism could work for or against such dysfunctional processes.[7]

By considering both the synergies and the dysfunctions that groups can develop, we can talk not only about "process losses" of groupthink, social loafing, and so on but also about "process gains" created in part from the range and diversity of alternative perspectives that are accrued from the diverse members and way the group goes about its business. The contribution of process to group effectiveness is shown in figure 7.1.

A key task for the manager of a multicultural team is therefore to maximize process gains and minimize process losses. This task is about facilitating cultural synergy (getting the benefits of the cultural differences in the group) and overcoming destructive cultural conflict or difference. The culturally intelligent manager must consider three ways in which culture influences group processes. As mentioned previously, the first of these involves the cultural norms and scripts for how groups function that each member brings to a group. The other two are the amount of *cultural diversity* that exists in the group and the *cultural distance* among group members.[8]

Cultural Diversity in Groups

A group is diverse—or *heterogeneous*—to the extent that its members are different from each other rather than similar to each other. Culture is only one dimension on which work group members are likely to differ; important others are gender, age, and experience. There is both good and bad news about the effect of diversity in work groups.

The bad news about diversity is that research has shown that it tends to have a negative effect on the way people feel about the group.[9] For example, members of a diverse group are more likely to be dissatisfied with the group and less likely to identify with it, which can lead to serious process losses.

Sometimes managers respond to this kind of difficulty by making a deliberate policy decision to try to avoid multicultural groups as far as possible. This is one way of accounting for the worldwide phenomenon of countries' taking in immigrants from culturally different overseas locations only to find that despite the immigrants' high qualifications, long experience, and strong work ethics, local companies simply prefer to employ less qualified local people. Local (low-CQ) managers tend to think that if they employ immigrants, they will suffer major process losses as the newcomers struggle to fit in. (In addition, of course, they may simply be prejudiced against them.)

To avoid process losses, some organizations have deliberate policies of making groups—particularly production groups—as homogeneous as possible. New Zealand, for example, has a high proportion of Samoan, Tongan, Cook Island, and other Pacific Island workers in the labor force of its cities. Some factories focus on a particular Island community as the basis of their workforces, or at least try to ensure that particular work teams or departments are made up of all Samoans or all Tongans. Although proponents of equal employment opportunity may not like such practices, some managers claim that they ensure there is no ethnic conflict and that each employee feels comfortable with his or her "mates." One Auckland businessman occasionally flies his all-Samoan workforce to Samoa at his own expense for a "family holiday," and his business is cited as a model of good employment.[10]

This approach is understandable, but it represents a short-term view. The process losses of diversity tend to be immediate, whereas the process gains of diversity take longer to show up. Effort and sensitivity shown in welcoming and orienting people who are different are likely to be rewarded later on, when the process losses disappear and process gains kick in.

This is the good-news side of the argument about diversity in work groups. The same research that shows that diversity has a negative impact on job satisfaction and identification also shows that diversity, at least in task-related skills, tends to be positively related to group performance in organizational settings.

This finding may be understood by considering what is likely to happen in a totally homogeneous group—that is, a group totally lacking in diversity, a group where members are all similar. For example, consider a task force trying to find the solution to a technical problem. They are all German. They are all male. They are all graduate engineers. They are all in their fifties. They all studied engineering at the same university, and they are all long-service employees in the chemical engineering department of the same company. You will probably agree that, competent as they may be, they are unlikely to come up with a range of different ideas relevant to the problem.

Diversity typically provides groups with a wider range of ideas and viewpoints. Like all forms of diversity, diversity in culture encourages diversity in ideas. Culturally different people have different worldviews. And the wider the range of ideas, the better the chance of finding good ones. Research shows that cultural diversity often results in more creative and higher-quality group decisions. This comes about not only because diversity means that more alternative viewpoints will be put forward but also because being conscious of cultural difference in the group focuses the group's attention on process issues, including listening to minority viewpoints.[11]

In addition, being culturally different might relate directly to the group task. In an increasingly globalized world, culturally different group members may be selected for groups precisely because of the unique knowledge they have about culturally different environments. For example, Brazilian or Indian members might be recruited to advise a European or Chinese company planning to export to Brazil or India, to provide information about the cultural or local-market features of their countries that may affect the campaign.

Cultural Distance in Groups

Another important factor in diverse groups is the *relative cultural distance* of group members. Cultural distance refers to how different each group member feels from each other group member.[12] For example, an Indonesian in a group with an American, a Canadian, and an Australian will feel much more distant from the other group members than they do from each other. When we are very different from other people in a group, it is noticeable to them and to us.

People who are somewhat culturally different from others in the group find it easier to become involved in group activities than those who are *very* culturally different. People are often aware of the great effort involved in overcoming extreme cultural differences. Rather than trying to cross what may be seen as an unbridgeable gap, they may prefer to withdraw from the group and keep their views to themselves. This happened to José in our opening case, in which the group was dominated by two Westerners. If members withdraw, their potential to assist the group is wasted. Group leaders need to decide how to respond to such a situation: for example, should they transfer a culturally distant person to another group where she or he will feel more at home, or should they focus their energy on bridging the cultural gap?

Summarizing research findings about diversity in teams, we can say that diversity provides a team with greater potential for excellence than does homogeneity. But because of the process-loss phenomenon, the risks are also higher that the group will founder.

Culturally Intelligent Group Management

The existence of diversity in a group does not guarantee the kind of creativity suggested above; it merely makes it possible. The task of the manager or group leader is to facilitate a process that will allow the creative side of diversity to flourish. Culturally intelligent people can do three things to reduce or eliminate process losses and to capitalize on diversity. These are to manage the environment of the group, to allow culturally diverse groups to develop, and to foster cultural intelligence in the group.

MANAGING THE GROUP ENVIRONMENT

The functioning of any group also depends on the managerial environment—management support, rewards, group status, and opportunities for self-management—within which it functions.

Management Support. Any group requires good management support, in the form of such things as material resources, relevant information, and psychological support shown as goodwill and respect. Cross-cultural groups especially need to work in an organization where management respects cultural difference and appreciates the potential that diversity offers to improve the organization's creativity and performance. A culturally intelligent team leader attempting to capitalize on cultural diversity in the way we have described is likely to fail if external management (particularly senior management) is seen to operate in a different way.

Rewards. As demonstrated by the case at the beginning of chapter 4, individualists like to be rewarded on the basis of their own contributions. In other words, they believe rewards should be equitable. Collectivists in some cases like to be rewarded on the basis of equal shares for all contributing to the group; they believe rewards should be equal. This sounds like an impossible problem for those who have to decide how rewards should be allocated to members of a multicultural group. Devising individualized pay systems rewarding each according to preference is impractical. And culturally diverse groups may develop their own consensus about an appropriate balance of individual and group rewards. However, virtually all of the research on this topic suggests that high-performing groups in any culture derive a substantial proportion of their rewards from group activities.[13]

Group Status. Most managers understand that, regardless of cultural composition, a group's high status in an organization will increase members' self-esteem. However, the extent to which this is true is also dependent on cultural differences: it is a matter of the place of the group in the individual's life. In some (primarily collectivist) cultures, it is a family group that is important to the individual above all others, so the work group is of much less importance. People in these cultures may care little about the status of the work group.

Self-Management. Providing objectives or general direction for groups—especially for teams—and allowing them to self-manage by finding their own processes for reaching their objectives is an option for the managers of any organization. It is an option that is increasingly fashionable when work is outsourced or contracted out. Research suggests that self-management has advantages for many teams, cross-cultural or not. For cross-cultural teams, it has the additional advantage of enabling team leaders to develop unique group processes for overcoming the specific cross-cultural issues of the team, without interference from the outside.

DEVELOPMENT OF CULTURALLY DIVERSE GROUPS

A key element of group development is the selection and allocation of members. Team leaders usually have some discretion—moderated perhaps by legislation or local policies pertaining to equal employment opportunity—to encourage or discourage diversity as they hire new staff or allocate staff members to particular groups. Such decisions need to be the product of careful consideration of issues covered earlier in this book. For example, are you prepared to accept and manage the likely short-term process losses of greater diversity in order to benefit from the prospective longer-term process gains?

One option is simply to wait for the group to develop on its own. Research shows that newly formed culturally diverse groups reduce their process losses over time by finding ways of working together better. However, in today's fast-paced world, waiting for group development to occur on its own is probably not good enough. Culturally diverse groups often need feedback about the effectiveness of the processes they are using. In many cases this feedback is best presented from outside the group. Cultural intelligence helps managers strike the right balance between delegation and direction.

The best way to capitalize on cultural diversity in groups is to try to ensure that group members have high CQ and group leaders have the will and the skills to explore process issues within the group. To facilitate the development of CQ, training group members in cross-cultural understanding and skills is valuable.

All group members can benefit from understanding the concepts presented in this book. Also, encouraging each member to talk either in formal meetings or in day-to-day conversation about his or her cultural background and its effects is good. A colleague of ours calls this process of understanding the similarities and differences among group members "mapping."[14] Of course care must be taken to avoid making comments that are judgmental. Using this book by working through cultural issues on a chapter-by-chapter basis or encouraging members to consider whether they can identify with characters in any of the case studies may also be a source of productive discussion.

The key element in exploring process issues is the provision of feedback to group members, both from each other and from observers outside the group. By coming to a good understanding of the dynamics within the group and the causes of its difficulties, group members can develop new productive ways of changing both their scripts for the group and their own behavior in it.

Virtual Multicultural Groups

A type of work group that is becoming increasingly important is the virtual team (or electronically mediated group) composed of people who do not necessarily meet face-to-face. Such groups are made possible by advances in information technology, including teleconferencing, videoconferencing, e-mail, collaborative software, and intranet-Internet systems. Globalization, plus the fact that the output of more and more teams is in the form of information or decisions rather than products or services, makes such teams ever more common. These groups may be geographically dispersed, with members located around the world. Groups like these solve some of the problems of face-to-face multicultural groups but create others.

THE NEW-PRODUCT DEVELOPMENT TEAM

New Tech is one of the top producers of technology manufacturing equipment in Canada. Its employees have access to a wide range of communications technology, including videoconferencing, teleconferencing, telephone, voice mail, e-mail, and fax. The New-Product Development Team (NPD) has been formed to manage a strategic alliance with a competitor in France. The companies are codeveloping products using components from each company, and they have cross-selling agreements. The team decides on product specifications and is responsible for contract implementation and service. Both companies' products require extensive engineering service, which makes the team members' tasks highly interdependent. According to one team member, "A problem with a customer's equipment could arise anywhere in the world at any time, and we might have to fix it using engineers from both companies at the same time."

The team is composed of eight members, three from the Canadian headquarters (including team leader Jean-Luc Dandurand), three more New Tech members from Western Europe (France, England, and Benelux), and the remaining two from the French partner. Three of the team members do not speak English fluently. The team has moderate cultural diversity. Strong differences have existed with regard to assumptions about whether members were responsible to the group or to themselves and whether careful planning or quick action was preferable.

The team has met in regular two-day face-to-face meetings every two months for the first year and now meets every three months. In addition to clarifying miscommunications and making major decisions, the face-to-face meetings allow members to develop strong interpersonal relationships. Between the meetings, the members exchange information frequently (more than twice a day on average) with at least five other team members. The first preference for communication is telephone, followed by e-mail and fax. Not all members have reliable access to e-mail, and some prefer to use it only for very simple information.

The performance outcomes of this team have been mixed. The team has not performed up to either company's expectations, and the project is behind schedule. However, given that this is the first attempt at such a venture by either company, team members and management feel that getting this far is a major accomplishment. Product development quality is high, and customer response is good.

Jean-Luc says, "This project has had a lot of struggles. Sometimes we're behind, and they [the French partner] have the upper hand; sometimes they're behind and we have the upper hand. But we're all learning, and we're getting better, and we've had enough success in a very tough market that we intend to just keep going."[15]

The product development team described above is typical of global virtual teams. In fact, it may be that in today's environment all teams work on a virtual basis at least part of the time. As shown in the case, effective global virtual teams need to fit their communication patterns to the task. Face-to-face communication is often interspersed with the periods of remote communication.

In virtual teams, many of the normal cues of interpersonal communication are reduced or removed, so cross-cultural differences, including language differences, are less noticeable. Yet because it may be harder to examine group processes and cultural differences, problems relating to cultural variables may be increased. Some people feel uncomfortable using electronic forms of communication, particularly if the information being conveyed is complex, novel, or subtle. The development of trust is more difficult when individuals have to work with others whom they cannot see or hear directly, and groups therefore tend to go through their developmental stages more slowly.

These are not reasons for avoiding geographically dispersed multicultural groups—again, information technology bestows a great boon by allowing groups to interact across enormous distances. But managers of such groups must be even more patient than usual and must create opportunities to introduce the missing characteristics of normal group functioning to the team. Some of the keys to overcoming the difficulties of geographic dispersion (virtuality) are:

- developing a shared understanding among group members about goals and group processes
- using information technology to integrate member skills and abilities
- fitting communication patterns to the task
- developing trust among group members[16]

Making Multicultural Work Groups More Effective

Clearly the existence and extent of multicultural work groups in any organization depends on factors external to the manager: for example, the composition of the available labor force, the hiring and firing policies of the organization, and top management support for diversity.

However, most people who have to lead and supervise multicultural groups have little influence over these matters and have to accept each situation as they find it and do their best to make it productive. Many situations may be multicultural, but every situation is unique. This means managers require not just CQ but also the knowledge and ability to perceive and take account of the specifics of the group situation. For example, it is vital for the manager to figure out

- whether the group is a team, a task force, or a crew
- whether the team faces relatively routine or relatively complex tasks

- the degree of cultural diversity in the group, the specific cultural issues, and whether the group has come to terms with these issues

- whether the group has a natural process for surfacing and dealing with cross-cultural issues and for ensuring that all group members contribute, regardless of their cultural origins

Our analysis suggests that there may well be some culturally diverse groups that, because of the nature of their task or because they have found their own ways of functioning effectively, require little deliberate action to stimulate their cross-cultural understanding.

However, there will be other groups, particularly teams and perhaps task forces, that require interpersonal sensitivity and working closely together on complex tasks. Here, the leader/manager must be proactive in assisting the group to examine, confront, and improve its own processes. Cultural scripts can be so diverse and so embedded in team members that resolution requires a major effort. However, the development of cultural intelligence in the team leader and team members can create a basis for mutual understanding and respect that will enable people to find their own ways to solve problems. Also, whatever the cultural mix, many of the techniques involved are in any case part and parcel of effective group leadership. In multicultural groups, the combination of CQ and team process skills can be a winning one.

Summary

Groups are in fashion. The popularity of team-based work environments, coupled with increasingly multicultural workforces, makes the ability to get the most from culturally diverse work teams an important current issue. In order to effectively manage or participate in multicultural work groups and teams, individuals need cultural knowledge, but also knowledge of group types, group tasks, and group structure and processes. In order for these work groups to function effectively, the group itself must develop cultural intelligence. Culturally diverse groups have the potential both for higher achievement and for greater failure than single-culture groups. The trick that they must perform is to maximize the positive effects of cultural diversity while at the same time minimizing its negative effects. This goal is achievable by high-CQ leaders who also use group-process knowledge, practice mindfulness in group interactions, adapt behavior to accommodate the unique circumstances of the group, and encourage and train members to become culturally intelligent as well.

Developing Cultural Intelligence in a Global World

THE BULL IN THE CHINA SHOP

Barbara Bull, an American public relations officer in a Beijing hotel, was annoyed with Weixing Li, a Chinese member of her staff, because Weixing had turned up late for an important assignment.

"Do you know what you did wrong?"

His response was a blank stare.

"Do you know what you did wrong? Do you know why I am upset?"

Another blank look.

"Don't you even know what you have done wrong?"

"Whatever you say I did wrong, I did wrong," he replied.

Barbara was taken aback. Was he being a smart aleck? "I want you to tell me what you did wrong!" she said.

"Whatever you say I did wrong, I did wrong. You are the boss. I'm sure whatever you say is correct. So whatever you say I did wrong, I will admit to."

This response made her even angrier. So she told him exactly what he had done wrong, describing his irresponsibility, immaturity, and failure. He apologized and said no more. He looked downcast. Did he understand the problem? Would he change his behavior?

Barbara had a subsequent conversation with her fellow manager Chrissie, who has been in China for several years. When Barbara described what had happened, Chrissie nodded.

"It's a common problem. You need to understand how important *mianzi* is to Chinese people."

"*Mianzi*? What's that?"

"We would call it 'face,' as in 'saving face' or 'losing face.' *Mianzi* is the motivating force behind a lot of actions in Chinese culture. You see, Chinese employees see things from a hierarchical viewpoint. Weixing probably knew he had done something wrong, but his way of handling it would have been to let his boss point out what he should have done differently. I'm afraid you made him lose face, which is bad for his commitment to the company. The good thing is, you didn't reprimand him in front of others. But in his eyes the loss of face would apply not just to him but to you. What you should have done was to highlight how his actions had caused you and the company to lose face. That would have caused him shame, and he would learn."

"Wow! I'll try to remember that next time I want to blow my top. But being in a foreign country is like walking on eggshells. People's egos are so easily crushed. How am I supposed to know these things? How do I learn to get it right? How can I practice?"

The case presents a paradox of cultural intelligence—a paradox that it shares with many other areas of human development. The paradox is this:

> In order to acquire cultural intelligence you must practice, by living and working in culturally different environments, or by working with culturally different people.

But

> In order to live and work effectively in culturally different environments, or to work successfully with culturally different people, you first need to acquire cultural intelligence.

This problem is a difficult one. In practice, it means that Barbara and Weixing and people like them must do two things at once: continuously observe and learn cultural intelligence at the same time as they do their day-to-day work. Barbara focused too intently on getting Weixing to diagnose his own error, and Weixing held on to his Chinese beliefs about hierarchical employee-employer relationships. Perhaps both will learn enough from this encounter for it to transfer to the next intercultural situation. And by sharing the problem with an experienced colleague, Barbara has been able to add an important element to the knowledge component of her cultural intelligence. This aspect of the case reminds us that cultural intelligence is not developed through mere exposure to other cultures but requires conscious effort.

Let's recap the concept of cultural intelligence. In its broadest sense, cultural intelligence is the capability to interact effectively with people from different cultural backgrounds. Cultural intelligence is composed of many facets. Cultural intelligence enables us to recognize cultural differences through knowledge and mindfulness, and it gives us an ability to act appropriately across cultures. The culturally intelligent person draws on a breadth of experience and can choose subtly different behaviors that perfectly fit the situation.

Characteristics Supportive of Cultural Intelligence

Some characteristics that individuals already possess or can develop make them more motivated and better able to increase their cultural intelligence. For example, personality characteristics such as openness to new experience, extroversion, and agreeableness relate positively to effective intercultural interaction. These traits improve the capacity for acquiring the skills required for culturally intelligent behavior. Again, mindfulness is key. This awareness, combined with the active pursuit of opportunities for cross-cultural interaction, lays a foundation for developing a high level of cultural intelligence.

Developmental Stages of CQ

The development of cultural intelligence occurs in several stages.

Stage 1: Reactivity to external stimuli. A starting point is a mindless adherence to one's own cultural rules and norms. This stage is typical of individuals with very little exposure to, or interest in, other cultures. These people may not even recognize that cultural differences exist, or they may consider them inconsequential. They may say things like "I don't see differences. I treat everyone the same."

Stage 2: Recognition of other cultural norms and motivation to learn more about them. Experience and mindfulness produce a new awareness of the multicultural mosaic that surrounds us. The individual is curious and wants to learn more. People at this stage often struggle with the complexity of the cultural environment. They search for simple rules of thumb to guide their behavior.

Stage 3: Accommodation of other cultural norms and rules in one's own mind. Reliance on absolutes disappears. A deeper understanding of cultural variation begins to develop. Different cultural norms and rules of conduct begin to seem comprehensible and even reasonable in their context. The individual knows what to say and do in different cultural situations but finds it difficult to adapt and is often awkward.

Stage 4: Assimilation of diverse cultural norms into alternative behaviors. At this stage, adjusting to different situations no longer requires much effort. Individuals develop a repertoire of behaviors from which they can choose depending on the specific cultural situation. They function in different cultures effortlessly, almost as if they were in their home cultures. Members of other cultures accept them as culturally knowledgeable and feel comfortable interacting with them. They feel at home almost anywhere.

Stage 5: Proactivity in cultural behavior based on recognition of changing cues that others do not perceive. People are able to sense changes in cultural context, sometimes even before members of the other culture. They are so attuned to the nuances of intercultural interactions that they automatically adjust their behavior to anticipate these changes and know how to execute the appropriate behavior effectively. Such individuals may be quite rare, but they demonstrate a level of cultural intelligence to which we might all aspire.

Culturally intelligent people have a *cognitively complex* perception of their environment. They are able to make connections between seemingly disparate pieces of information. They describe people and events in terms of many different characteristics and are able to see the many links among these characteristics. They can see a coherent pattern in a cultural situation.

Culturally intelligent individuals are able to see past the stereotypes that a superficial understanding of cultural dimensions—such as collectivism, uncertainty avoidance, and power distance (see chapter 2)—provide. Knowledge of these dimensions is only a first step in developing cultural intelligence.[1] Culturally intelligent people see the connections between a culture and its context, history, and values.

The Process of Developing Cultural Intelligence

As outlined in chapter 1, cultural intelligence involves three components—knowledge, mindfulness, and skills. Raising your CQ requires experiential learning that can take considerable time. It requires a base level of knowledge, the acquisition of new knowledge and alternative perspectives through mindfulness, and the development of this knowledge into behavioral skills. The process is iterative and can be thought of as a series of S curves, as shown in figure 8.1.[2]

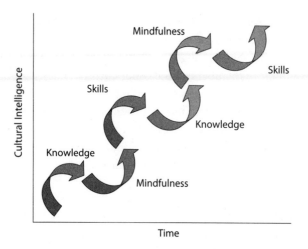

FIGURE 8.1. The development of cultural intelligence

The acquisition of cultural intelligence involves learning from social interactions. Such social learning is a very powerful way in which people's experiences are transferred into knowledge and skills.[3] Social learning involves *attention* to the situation, *retention* of the knowledge gained from the situation, *reproduction* of the behavioral skills observed, and finally *reinforcement* (receiving feedback) about the effectiveness of the adapted behavior.

Improving CQ by learning from social experience means paying attention to, and appreciating, critical differences between oneself and others in culture and background. This requires some knowledge about the ways in which cultures differ and how culture affects behavior. It also requires us to be mindful of contextual cues and open to the legitimacy and importance of different behavior. To retain this knowledge, we need to be able to transfer what we learn from a specific experience to later interactions in other settings. To reproduce the skills, we need to practice them in future interactions. To reinforce the skills, the more frequently and mindfully we try out behaviors and are successful, the more quickly cultural intelligence improves.

As implied by figure 8.1, improving your CQ takes time, and you must be motivated to do it. The iterative and long-term nature of gaining cultural intelligence is illustrated in the following example.

UNDERSTANDING THE FRENCH

Jenny Stephens is a thirty-five-year-old U.S. national working as an executive for the French subsidiary of an American multinational. After meeting and marrying a Frenchman in New York, she moved to Paris, where she has lived for seven years. She speaks French fluently and interacts with French relatives and friends and colleagues on a regular basis. When asked if she feels she understands French culture, she says,

> I have been here for seven years. In an almost predictable manner, I have found that whenever I would begin to get a sense that I really understand the French, something strange would happen that would throw me off completely. As I would reflect on the event and talk it over with my husband and friends, I would begin to develop a more complex view of the French. Then, things would go fine for several months until the whole process would repeat itself in some other area.
>
> For example, I really felt I was making progress when I learned how to buy cheese. Putting together a proper cheese plate in France is at least as complicated as choosing wine correctly. A perfect cheese presentation must contain five cheeses—a ripe (but not too ripe) light, soft cheese; a hard, sharp cheese; a goat cheese; a semisoft cheese; and a blue cheese. However, just knowing this is insufficient to be viewed as anything but a novice in a French cheese shop. To be truly expert, one must know what cheeses from what regions are particularly good at the moment. When I learned that by simply using my base-level knowledge and asking appropriate questions such as what brie is particularly good this week, I was treated with much more respect.[4]

In this case Jenny is practicing a kind of mindfulness by recognizing unusual things that she observes as being related to culture and talking them over with her husband and friends. She also uses mindfulness when she recognizes that her limited knowledge can be used effectively by planning how to adapt her behavior. In this way, each instance of idiosyncratic French behavior builds on her previous knowledge and contributes to her development of cultural intelligence.

Activities That Support the Development of Cultural Intelligence

Perhaps the most important means of increasing cultural intelligence is spending time in foreign countries, during which cross-cultural experiences will be frequent and CQ will increase through necessity. While foreign experiences are ideal, there are numerous other situations and activities you can draw upon to increase cultural intelligence. These range from formal education to various informal interactions. For many people, the opportunity and motivation to become more culturally intelligent come from developing a close relationship with someone who is culturally different.

The activities outlined below can be important for developing cultural intelligence.

FORMAL EDUCATION/TRAINING

The types of formal training available to help you improve your CQ can be classified according to the extent that they are experience-based (as opposed to purely "classroom") and the extent to which they are culture-specific or applicable across cultures. All of these types of training are valuable, but, as we suggested in chapter 1, true cultural intelligence requires learning from experience and building knowledge that develops skills that can be applied across cultures. The following chart shows the types of formal training available and how they apply to our model of developing a high CQ.

TRAINING TYPE	TRAINING METHOD	APPLICATION TO CQ
Factual	Books, lectures, films, area briefings	Knowledge about specific cultures, culture dimensions, and processes
Analytical	Case study analysis, discussion, culture assimilators (self-administered, programmed culture-training manuals)	Both culture-general and culture-specific knowledge as well as the opportunity to practice mindfulness
Experiential	Simulations, role-playing, field trips, actual inter-cultural experience (at home or abroad)	Opportunities to practice both mindfulness and behavior skills, and to experience the emotions of cross-cultural interaction

Of the three types of methods, experiential training is the most rigorous and effective in developing a high CQ. But formal experiential training is rare and often expensive. To become culturally intelligent, therefore, most of us rely on our day-to-day interactions with people who are culturally different. Several contexts in which these interactions occur are worth mentioning here. These are cross-cultural teams, interactions with culturally different individuals at home, and foreign assignments.

CROSS-CULTURAL GROUPS AND TEAMS

As discussed in chapter 7, the world's work is performed by groups or teams. Additionally, most people are involved in social and interest groups. Because of globalization, such groups are increasingly composed of people from different cultures. As well as being a management challenge, multicultural groups offer a rich opportunity for all of us to gain cultural intelligence without necessarily leaving our own country. Culturally diverse groups offer us the opportunity to observe the behavior of individuals from different cultures responding to the same situations—for example, the assignment of group roles, the establishment of a leader, the imposition of deadlines, and all the other activities and processes of working in a group. Also, if we are mindful, we will note the wide variety of reactions from culturally different members to their own group's behavior. The interactions of culturally different people in groups are complex, but that complexity generates great learning opportunities. Thus, diversity within the groups we engage in should be seen not as a threat but as an opportunity for us to develop greater cultural intelligence by using role models.

CROSS-CULTURAL INTERACTIONS AT HOME

Our multicultural societies may present us with numerous opportunities to engage with others who are culturally different. However, these interactions are often superficial and lack the depth and intensity that is required for us to enjoy experiential learning. For a Westerner, having dinner at a Cantonese restaurant and interacting with the service people is indeed an intercultural experience, but it is a very mild one (although it might become a bit more intense with an order of chicken feet!) and lacks significant engagement. In the same way that leadership skills are often taught by means of challenging outdoor activities such as ropes courses, significant CQ development requires us to move outside our comfort zone and to challenge ourselves in deeper ways than a restaurant experience allows.

In our international management courses we, the authors, routinely require our students to engage in a nontrivial cross-cultural experience in their local area in order to practice the skills they have learned in class. "Culture" in this case is not confined to national or ethnic culture but, consistent with our definition in chapter 2, can be any social group. Subcultures in a society provide excellent learning experiences. We tell students that if they are to learn, they should feel culturally uncomfortable in the situation, at least at first. Some ways to engage in cross-cultural experiences are:

- Attend a religious service or wedding ceremony of someone from another culture. Ask a member of the culture to explain the significance of the rituals involved.

- Locate an ethnic organization in your community and attend (and participate in, if possible) a cultural celebration. Ask members to explain the significance of the event and the symbolism of the activities.

- Find an interest group that represents a set of beliefs to which you do not subscribe and attend one of its meetings. For example, some of our heterosexual university students have attended meetings of gay and lesbian associations. One of our mature executive students attended "drum and bass night" at a nightclub with her son — a major excursion into an unfamiliar youth culture. The following is an excerpt from her report.

DRUM & BASS NIGHT AT THE LOTUS CLUB

For my cross-cultural experience, I went to "drum & bass night" at the Lotus Club on Abbott Street. The Lotus is one of Vancouver's underground rave-type clubs. Ordinarily, I really would not have known such clubs existed. And certainly I would never have considered actually going into one. But as it happens, my son, who is a jazz musician, is visiting right now, and he offered (as a joke, I think) to take me. I leapt at the opportunity to find out something about his world as well as fulfill my course requirements. I lost some of my enthusiasm when I found out what time the event took place (beginning at 11:00 p.m.) and what it involved.

The Lotus Hotel . . . looks really old, beer stained, maybe opium stained, with a kind of elemental grime I associate with the New York subway covering every surface . . . .

There's a way people look when they sleep all day and get up at 7:00 or 8:00 p.m. and go out at night. They get a night-person look.

The sound was so intense that at first it was an effort to walk towards it, to actually penetrate the wall of cigarette smoke and noise. Once inside it was more like a bath of music, wave after wave, pulsating, the walls were moving, the room was moving, everything was moving. I could feel a sensation like a force rhythmically pressing my chest. . . . I realized I was tensing every muscle as though resisting a blow and found if I relaxed into it, it became a lot easier, even sort of energizing.

The dancers were incredible—moves like you see on TV. . . . The music didn't seem to have a beginning or end, either. It just went on and on. . . .

[Their] outfits had that air of being carefully chosen to represent something—I just didn't know what it was.

I felt very conspicuous. My main reaction was to get into a corner, almost to hide. I wanted to watch without being noticed.

I felt overwhelmed. After a while, those feelings went away and were replaced by a kind of sadness. . . .

I could have danced, I guess, but I would have looked ridiculous. At least I thought I would look ridiculous. I felt like a foreigner, someone who would not be welcome and would somehow interrupt the flow. . . . There was no way I belonged in that group.

As more people showed up, I began to feel nervous. Some people looked strange and menacing, with leather, tattoos, body piercing in places I found to be weird.

I felt like I needed a friend in this cold, loud, unfamiliar world. I caught a few glimpses of my son as he flitted from here to there, dancing, drinking beer, and talking to people. Finally, he said, "Let's go home."

I was really happy to see the outside world. . . . I've done my fair share of traveling and even lived abroad for four years. [This experience] reminded me that there is a lot going on around me that I don't know about. And, I do think I experienced a little, tiny bit of what it's like to have to function in a distant culture, where nothing is as usual, and even things that seem familiar turn out to be strange.

This adult student's observation of the Lotus Club is a good example of mindfulness in action and the development of cultural intelligence. The uncomfortable situation made it difficult for the student to operate on cultural cruise control, but the vivid description of the situation shows an acute attention to the behavior of the culturally different others and the context. Also, this case shows that cross-cultural interactions can be found in your own backyard as well as outside your country's borders.

FOREIGN EXPERIENCE AND EXPATRIATE ASSIGNMENTS

One of the most challenging ways of confronting cultural differences is living and working in a foreign country for a temporary period.

BUT I AM CHINESE!

A Chinese American, with a master's degree in international business and fluency in Chinese, has taken an overseas assignment in China working for a multinational firm. She feels she will be a bridge between the Chinese and American managers in the firm. However, she is surprised when she realizes that she has misunderstood the work environment in China. A year into the assignment, she notes: "My understanding of managing effectively came primarily from trial and error. I learned the hard way, falling on my face. But each time I fell, I'd assess what the critical learning of each incident was. I think that one must have an open mind when accepting an overseas assignment. China has one of the highest expatriate assignment failure rates in the world. I believe that the lack of ability to manage across cultures is at the top of the list of reasons. And the reason for this is that expatriates fail to understand the thought processes and motivation of local employees."[5]

This case demonstrates that cultural intelligence is often gained by trying out new behaviors and observing their effect.

Learning from each cross-cultural interaction, even if it doesn't always work out as planned, is an important way to improve cultural intelligence. Also, the observation of the protagonist that understanding how local employees think is important to expatriate success cannot be overemphasized. Foreign visits and assignments, perhaps more than any situation, require that you try to understand the behavior of others in terms of their own cultural background. This situation too offers you opportunities for intense experiential learning. If, like most people, you have had very little cross-cultural training before going overseas, you will have to adjust "on the fly."

In foreign experience, unlike working in teams, we are typically focused on the single culture in which we are immersed. Because of this immersion the experience tends to be intense and emotionally charged. Living in a foreign culture may cause high stress levels until we adjust. When everything and everyone seem to be working against us, it is difficult to see the situation as a meaningful learning experience.

Figure 8.2 shows a model of the phases that some experts believe people go through as they adjust to a foreign environment.[6] The process follows a U-shaped curve through a honeymoon period, culture shock, attempted adjustment, and then mastery. In the honeymoon stage everything is new and exciting, as it would be to a short-term tourist. In fact, fast-moving tourists may never get beyond this stage, making tourism often too shallow an experience for the acquisition of very much cultural intelligence. In the culture-shock stage, the differences between what the expatriate is used to and what the new culture provides become apparent, as the individual either learns—including developing his or her CQ—or fails to learn how to adapt. Those with high CQ get into the routines and rhythms of daily life in the new country and move eventually to a position of mastery, while others may never properly adjust.

A real possibility for some people is that the adjustment is so successful and their view of the new country so positive

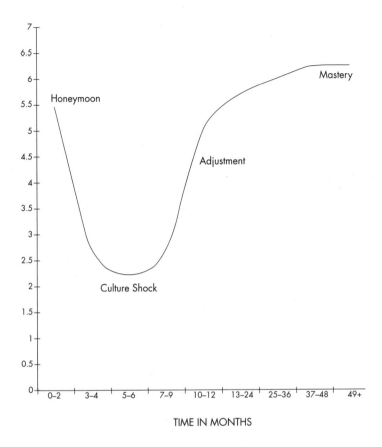

FIGURE 8.2. The U-curve of cross-cultural adjustment

that they lose all desire to return home. Others meet romantic partners in the new environment, and the couple must make the tough decision about which of them will make the other's country home.

GOING NATIVE

As he looked out from the top-floor restaurant over Lake Michigan and the magnificent Chicago skyline, Yukimichi (Mike) Kusumoto thought about how his expatriate assignment to the United States had turned into a permanent move. Like many Japanese, initially he had had great difficulty adjusting to the extreme foreignness of the United States. The crime-rate statistics were so frightening that he came to Chicago without his wife, Naoko, and family, intending to accomplish his assignment and then return to his firm back in Japan. However, what was even more frightening when he arrived was the amazing diversity in America. The sheer variety of people and cultures in Chicago was startling. And at the office he had initially been frustrated by the short-sightedness of his colleagues, their failure to treat customers as honored guests, and their use of lawyers to protect themselves from their own hasty decisions. Yes, adjusting to the United States had been very difficult.[7]

He couldn't say exactly when he began to feel more comfortable in Chicago than back in Tokyo. Of course his English was now very good, and Naoko had joined him after a year and had eventually integrated well into American society. By carefully observing and trying to understand American business practices, he had finally been very successful at work—so successful that a competing American company had eventually recruited him at a much higher salary. Even though he had insisted that his two daughters go to the special Japanese school in the Chicago suburb where they lived, they were now as American as they were Japanese—not a bad thing, he thought. Now he expected that they would attend an American university rather than go back to Japan. For himself, Yukimichi had grown to appreciate the American way of life. He enjoyed its freedoms and spontaneity and loved his spacious home and beautiful neighborhood—such a contrast with the tiny apartment he had left in Tokyo. He had even found himself admiring the independence of Americans, and he did his best to act that way himself. It seemed to suit his personality. Go back to Japan? No, he was an American now.

Cultural intelligence may be important for the whole family. If you want your children to grow up with a high CQ in a world that will increasingly value it, why not give them a taste of international experience while they are still young and flexible enough to make the most of it? They will need support and guidance, but it will be a great opportunity—gaining cultural intelligence as a family experience.

For those of us in international organizations, our employers can assist adjustment to overseas postings by providing appropriate training. There is evidence that cross-cultural training assists overseas adjustment, relationships with host nationals, and employee performance. However, some organizations believe cross-cultural training is not effective and do not provide it. If you have been given this book by your company as part of an education program, this is a sign that the company is giving some thought to these important issues.

The nature of careers is changing, making traditional company-sponsored overseas assignments unavailable to many. However, these assignments are only one of many types of international opportunities available.

DOING IT HER WAY

Margaret is English. She has always enjoyed travel. At nineteen, she traveled for two years in Europe, spending time particularly in Greece and Ireland. She funded her travel mainly by working as a bartender, and in Greece even gained supervisory experience in a restaurant. Her experience in Greece sparked an interest in history, and she has always had an interest in business. So on her return to the UK, she went to university to study history and economics.

When she finished the degree, Margaret decided that she wanted a career in teaching. But she was restless and wanted to go traveling again first, perhaps to Asia this time. So she applied for and gained a place with JET (Japanese Exchange Teaching)—teaching English to adults in Japan. She thought that the opportunity would be culturally valuable to her and would enable her to try teaching and to save money. She hoped to see a lot of Asia, learn to speak Japanese, develop some teaching skills, and save a nest egg to take home. Her assignment was in Osaka, with a contract for two years.

Margaret soon settled into the JET work in Osaka. JET rules stipulated that the organization's employees were not permitted to take other work, but Margaret was soon approached by a local government organization wanting to hire her to set up an English-language program for its employees. She thought this opportunity would enable her to gain further personal and professional development. JET turned a blind eye. The part-time work lasted six months, and the evening teaching it involved was interesting, as the students were keen to learn English. Also, the cost of living was such that she needed the additional income in order to earn her nest egg. And it put her into a friendly social circle and enabled her to take trips and see Japan with the adult students.

Margaret had enough money and time away from teaching to do about three months' touring per year in Asia. She traveled with an American boyfriend, who was a colleague in the JET program. Other social contacts were Mama-san and Papa-san—a café-owner couple with whom she boarded. They adopted her, almost as if she were their own daughter. They showed her around, taught her about Japanese ways, communicated with her only in Japanese, and gave her part-time work in the café. Margaret's cultural learning was dramatic.

After two years, Margaret was offered an extension of her JET contract, but she wanted to return to Britain. She knew she wanted to live there, she wanted to see her parents and brothers again, and she wanted to own her own home. She had broken off her relationship with her American boyfriend.

She still would have liked to teach. But she thought about the negative attitudes and poor self-discipline of British school students and compared them unfavorably to those of her Japanese students. The Japanese were so polite and motivated compared with British pupils. She realized how poorly paid teachers were. She returned to the UK with some money but no real plan apart from a vague desire to get into management. She bought a small house in her home city.

She got a job as a sales rep for a company selling print and database solutions and soon realized that she had found her forte—selling. Then she was approached by her present employer, a software company, and took a sales job with them. The job is good but doesn't take all her energy or fulfill all her interests. She aspires to be a manager, or, better still, would like to start her own business. She learned a thing or two from Mama-san and Papa-san and the way they had turned their little Osaka café into a gold mine! But she feels she lacks skills and knowledge relating to the wider business world, so she enrolled for a master's degree in business. She has a business plan—to start an export-based Internet company selling British products overseas. For this venture, she sees Japan as a key market and believes her understanding of the language and culture will assist her greatly.

Among the things Margaret learned overseas were the Japanese language (and a smattering of other Asian languages), patience, and what she calls "cultural sensitivity"—particularly how to interact with Asians, an ability she uses a lot in her current employment, where several of the staff are Indian or Chinese. She gained a heightened awareness of the importance of education, plenty of self-confidence, and a broader perspective than she had before. She also increased her drive: "It [the overseas experience] got me growing again—I caught up with my friends." She enhanced her cooking skills, her ability to speak in public, even her abilities in tennis and other sports, as well as judo. And of course she has a special interest in, and affinity for, Japan and its people, and good contacts there. She knows Japan will continue to be important in her life.

Margaret considers the most significant learning was about herself—who she was, what her skills were, what she wanted to do. But the appreciation of Japanese and Asian culture and its contrasts with Europe were also very important. She is very clear that there is no way she could have developed in the same ways by spending the two years in her familiar British cultural environment. Overall, Margaret says her time in Japan was "the best time of my life."[8]

In her determined internationalism, Margaret is typical of many of today's young people. Today's young people want to see the world. Employment in another culture forces the employee to come to grips with the culture. So, increasingly, people work as they travel, and the acquisition of cultural intelligence is integrated with their career development. Her experience is typical. As one returnee from extended foreign travel put it:

> I have learned to look at the world around me with a child-like wonder and to drop any preconceived notions I may have been holding. I have learned that just because I have grown up indoctrinated by a certain set of rules regarding how relationships and society in general work, that does not make them universally true or right.

If you are a middle-aged reader and are thinking, "Gee, I wish I had thought like that when I was young," it's never too late. Talk to your children about it!

ACQUIRING CQ THROUGH OVERSEAS EXPERIENCE

As shown above, spending time living and working abroad is an important way of developing cultural intelligence. But it will not happen automatically. You will have to prepare, focus, and be mindful. Every cross-cultural incident—at your work, in social life, even when shopping—will be an opportunity to reflect, to learn, and to experiment.

You will need to be in the right *frame of mind* to acquire CQ. Why are you going overseas? What do you want from the experience? Escaping a bad situation at home or hoping for career advancement on return may not be the best motivation. Self-development, a desire for adventure, a wish to broaden your horizons and meet new kinds of people, or a sense of mission are better. They will help you to live in the here-and-now and to take a genuine interest in your new environment and the people you meet.

You will need to *prepare*. Read all you can about the new country you are to visit. Find out about its cultural background, using literature like that recommended at the end of this book. Study the cultural dimensions we introduced in chapter 2, and try to figure out where your new home fits in. Seek out people who have been there, and ask them about their experiences.

In many foreign locations there are opportunities for incomers to feel at home—restaurants and communities set up by expatriates, international hotels modeled on Western norms and standards, even, for example in Saudi Arabia, compounds or housing developments designed for specific groups of foreigners. If you want to develop cultural intelligence, you should avoid the temptation of spending all your time in these environments: essentially they are just extensions of home. Remember our advice to "get out of your comfort zone," and seek experiences that are genuinely local.

Also remember that the most common reasons that people return early from overseas are family issues. Involve family members who are going overseas with you in the preparation, and support them in the adventure. It is their opportunity to acquire cultural intelligence too, and their adjustment is just as important as your own. For your children, an international move is a unique opportunity to grow CQ. Being young, they will have fewer fixed beliefs, less cultural cruise control. It is an ideal opportunity for them to learn quickly. However, children sometimes need guidance to avoid becoming completely absorbed in the new culture. They may need help in learning that the essence of cultural intelligence is to be able to respond to different cultural situations without losing one's own identity.

You will have to be self-forgiving and patient. Even with plenty of preparation, you will doubtless make many initial mistakes. Your performance in the first year abroad is unlikely to be your best. You will probably sometimes need to laugh at your own inadequacies and to remember that even the most negative experience holds potential for learning.

The future for many is not just intercultural but international. We, and our children, will more and more have to be able to feel at home wherever we are and to function with the ease and familiarity that is habitual to us on home soil. The opportunity to travel overseas is precious. The investment is our time and aspirations and the energy we give to the process. Part of the dividend we receive is enhanced cultural intelligence. As we hope this book has shown, the reward is well worth the effort.

Rules of Cross-Cultural Engagement

Lastly, regardless of the specific cultural context, there are several "rules of engagement" that you should try to keep in mind as you approach interactions with others who are culturally different. These are:

- Become knowledgeable about your own culture and background, its biases and idiosyncrasies, and the way these are unconsciously reflected in your own perceptions and behavior.

- Deliberately avoid mindlessness: expect differences in others. See different behavior as novel, and suspend evaluation of it.

- Switch into a mindful mode in which you are attentive to behavioral cues and their possible interpretations and the likely effect of your behavior on others.

- Adapt your behavior in ways that you are comfortable with and believe are appropriate for the situation.

- Be mindful of responses to your behavioral adaptation.

- Experiment with methods of adapting intuitively to new situations, and use these experiments to build your comfort level in acquiring a repertoire of new behaviors.

- Practice new behaviors that work until their production becomes automatic.

Summary

This chapter defines the concept of cultural intelligence as the capability to interact effectively with people from different cultural backgrounds. Developing cultural intelligence requires finding development experiences that involve both acquiring knowledge and applying mindfulness. In developing cultural intelligence, we go through a series of stages, from simply reacting to external stimuli to proactively adjusting behavior in anticipation of subtle changes in the cultural context. There are some underlying characteristics of individuals that support this development. Cultural intelligence can be developed in a number of ways, including formal education and training, but experiential learning is critical to the development of a high CQ. Our multicultural environment provides many opportunities for raising our CQ. Time spent living and working overseas is one of the best ways to improve cultural intelligence, but one should know a good deal about oneself before undertaking foreign experience, and one should understand the phenomenon of culture shock and the process of adjustment. Practicing mindfulness enhances this ability. Following a few simple guidelines for intercultural interactions can improve cultural intelligence and develop the ability to act competently across a wide range of cultures, adding an extremely valuable skill to your repertoire.

The Essentials
of Cultural Intelligence

The twenty-first century world is increasingly global, and the ability to deal effectively with others who are culturally different has become a daily necessity. This globalization is being fueled by dramatic economic shifts in many countries and by advances in communications technology. We may not travel the globe, but the world has come to us. Daily we have to deal with international issues and with people from other countries and cultures.

Despite rapid modernization, culture is slow to change. For the foreseeable future, cultural differences will remain a key factor in interpersonal interactions. And we have long known that in the organizations where we spend most of our time, interacting effectively with others is the most important part of our work lives. In an increasingly competitive world, individuals who do not keep their skills up to date run the risk of losing out. In this book, we have introduced what we believe to be a key competency for the twenty-first century: *cultural intelligence*. Cultural intelligence, the capability to deal effectively with people from different cultural backgrounds, is a multifaceted competency consisting of cultural *knowledge*, the practice of *mindfulness*, and a repertoire of *cross-cultural skills*.

In order to get a sense of your current level of cultural intelligence, ask yourself how well the following statements describe you:

- I know the ways in which cultures around the world are different.
- I can give examples of these differences from my personal experience, reading, and so on.
- I enjoy talking with people from different cultures.
- I have the ability to accurately understand the feelings of people from other cultures.
- I sometimes try to understand people from another culture by imagining how something looks from their perspective.
- I can change my behavior to suit different cultural situations and people.
- I accept delays without becoming upset.
- I am aware of the cultural knowledge I use when interacting with someone from another culture.
- I think a lot about the influence that culture has on my behavior and that of others who are culturally different.
- I am aware that I need to plan my course of action when in different cultural situations and with culturally different people.

The more these statements describe you, the higher your level of cultural intelligence is likely to be.[1]

As shown in figure 8.1, cultural intelligence is developed in an experiential, iterative way in which each repetition of the cycle builds on the previous one. The feedback from each cycle of experience leads to an ever-higher cultural intelligence quotient, or CQ. In this way, specific knowledge gained in both formal and informal ways is transformed into an ability that can then be applied to a variety of new situations.

Culture has a profound influence on almost all aspects

of human endeavor. The culturally intelligent person understands the possible effects of cultural variation on his or her
own behavior and that of others. The culturally intelligent
person also knows how and in what circumstances these cultural differences are likely to have an effect. Culture matters,
but it doesn't matter to the same degree in all circumstances
all the time.

Cultural intelligence also requires the practice of mindfulness. Mindfulness is being aware of our own assumptions,
ideas, and emotions; noticing what is apparent about the
other person's assumptions, words, and behavior; using all of
the senses in perceiving situations; viewing the situation from
several perspectives; attending to the context to help to interpret what is happening; creating new mental maps of others;
creating new and more sophisticated categories for others;
seeking out fresh information to confirm or disconfirm the
mental maps; and using empathy.

Knowledge and mindfulness are key elements of cultural
intelligence, but in themselves they are not enough. Becoming
culturally intelligent means acquiring cross-cultural skills. It
is not just about becoming more skilled but also about developing a repertoire of skilled behaviors and knowing when to
use each one. While everyone can learn to be culturally intelligent, certain characteristics of individuals, such as openness,
extraversion, and agreeableness support the development of
cultural intelligence.

- Culturally intelligent *decision makers* understand how
  people with different cultural backgrounds mentally simplify the complex decision-making process. They know
  their own motivation and goals in making decisions and
  understand how the motivations, goals, and decision-
  making methods of people from other cultures might be
  different from their own, and that cultural factors may
  sometime outweigh Western concepts of "rationality."
  They are mindful of the ethical components of business

decisions and the relationship of ethical behavior to their underlying cultural values. Finally, they are able to adapt decision behavior such as the type and amount of information gathered, the weighting of decision criteria, and the degree of participation in decisions to the specific cultural context, while at the same time respecting the universal rights of human beings.

- Culturally intelligent *communicators* and *negotiators* know that cultural differences have a huge influence on the communication process that underpins all negotiations. Managers spend much of their time in communication with others, and in no other activity is people's cultural grounding more influential. Both language and nonverbal behavior make it tricky to communicate across cultures. Culturally intelligent negotiators have the knowledge required to anticipate communication differences, practice mindfulness by paying attention to both the context and the conventions of communication as well as its content, and adapt their negotiation behavior to make concessions, persuade, exchange information, and/or build relationships as appropriate for the negotiation and cultural context.

- Culturally intelligent *leaders* know that leadership exists largely in the minds of followers. While all followers expect leaders to have a vision, to be able to communicate that vision, and to have skill in organizing followers, the specific behaviors that indicate these abilities vary dramatically across cultures. The culturally intelligent leader understands that his or her leadership style will be largely either task- or relationship-oriented but that some adaptation of this style may be required depending on the needs of followers (for example, their degree of collectivism). Culturally intelligent leaders do not unthinkingly mimic the leadership behaviors of another culture. Rather, they pay close attention to leaders like themselves who are effective in the cross-cultural environment and model their behavior appropriately.

- Culturally intelligent team members and team leaders know that culturally diverse work groups and teams have the potential for very high achievement but that they also have characteristics that make them prone to failure. The key to managing culturally diverse work groups lies in maximizing the benefits of diversity while at the same time minimizing the costs. Culturally intelligent team management also requires fostering cultural intelligence among team members. In order to do this, team members and team leaders must understand the effects of group processes as well as the steps to cultural intelligence. Team managers must consider the effects of group type, the nature of the group task, the degree and nature of the cultural diversity in the group, and the extent to which the group has developed the necessary internal processes to resolve conflict.

The development of cultural intelligence is an iterative process. Each intercultural interaction in which we engage offers the opportunity to enhance our cultural intelligence. Cultural intelligence can be developed here at home. However, for a person seeking cultural intelligence, a period of time living and working overseas, either self-initiated or as a company assignment, can be extremely rewarding.

We wish that we could somehow endow you with cultural intelligence or that you could download it from the Internet. But developing cultural intelligence involves hard work on your part. It is essentially an experiential process. As such it is often both physically and emotionally taxing. However, we think the feelings of confidence and control in cross-cultural interactions that you will feel are worth the effort. We hope this book has helped to start you on this journey.

Twenty Statements Test[1]

There are twenty numbered blanks on the next page. Please write twenty answers to the simple question "Who am I?" in the blanks. Just give twenty answers to this question. Answer as if you were giving the answers to yourself, not to somebody else. Write the answers in the order that they occur to you. Don't worry about logic or "importance." Go along fairly fast, as if time were limited.

WHO AM I?

1. _____

2. _____

3. _____

4. _____

5. _____

6. _____

7. _____

8. _____

9. _____

10. _____

11. _____

12. _____

13. _____

14. _____

15. _____

16. _____

17. _____

18. _____

19. _____

20. _____

Classify each statement into one of the following categories:

Independent: Statements about physical description, personal qualities, attitudes, beliefs, states, and traits that DO NOT relate to other people. Examples: "I am honest," "I am intelligent," "I am happy," "I have blue eyes," and so on.

Interdependent: Statements that relate to other people, such as social roles, interdependence, friendship, responsiveness to others, and sensitivity to how others perceive you. Examples: "I am a student," "I am a husband," "I am a member of the football team," "I am a person who wants to help others," and so on.

The number of items in each category can give you an idea of the extent to which you see yourself as *independent* from other people or *interdependent* with other people.

Where to Get Country Information

The purpose of this book is to help readers begin a journey toward a new way of thinking and being with respect to different cultures. However, we recognize that our "process view" of effective cross-cultural interaction by becoming *culturally intelligent* is based on some knowledge of specific cultural differences. Moreover, living and working in other countries often requires a deep understanding of economic, legal, and political conditions as well as culture. With this need in mind, we provide the following list of websites and book series. The dozen websites are those that we have found useful. Please note that they are biased toward U.S. and Canadian sites because these are the ones we use. There are comparable sites in other regions (particularly Europe) that offer similar information.

Also listed are book series that are devoted to helping people live and do business in specific countries or regions. These books have their place in developing cultural intelligence. However, we caution readers that the vast majority of these books are written from a Western perspective and may overlook certain critical aspects of cultural difference. Their content and depth of coverage vary widely. You should use these books with caution and expect that your own experience could be very different from that described.

Internet Sites

1. *Country Background Notes* (U.S. Department of State) Background Notes are factual publications that contain information on all the countries of the world with which the United States maintains relations. They include facts on the country's land, people, history, government, political conditions, and economy, and its relations with other countries and the United States. The Notes are updated and revised by the Office of Electronic Information and Publications of the Bureau of Public Affairs as they are received from regional bureaus and are added to the database of the Department of State website.

   http://www.state.gov/r/pa/ei/bgn/

2. *Country Commercial Guides* (U.S. Department of Commerce) The Country Commercial Guides (CCG) are prepared by U.S. embassy staff once a year and contain information on the business and economic situations of foreign countries and the political climates as they affect U.S. business. Each CCG contains the same chapter organization and an appendix and includes topics such as marketing, trade regulations, investment climate, and business travel. They can be found in the library section of the following webpage.

   http://www.export.gov/mrktresearch/index.asp

3. *Country Studies: Area Handbook Series* This website contains the online versions of books previously published in hard copy by the Federal Research Division of the Library of Congress under the Country Studies/Area Handbook Program sponsored by the U.S. Army. Because the original intent of the series sponsor was to focus primarily on lesser-known areas of the world or regions in which U.S.

forces might be deployed, the series is not all-inclusive. At present, 102 countries and regions are covered. Notable omissions include Canada, France, the United Kingdom, and other Western nations, as well as a number of African nations. The date of publication appears on the title page of the section for each country and at the end of each section of text. This site is a good source for information about non-Western countries but doesn't usually have current data. The material is useful as background information.

http://lcweb2.loc.gov/frd/cs/cshome.html

4. *Department of Foreign Affairs and International Trade (DFAIT; Canada): Market Reports* Through this site, DFAIT provides free access to hundreds of sectoral market studies and country-specific reports prepared by its Market Research Centre and by its offices abroad. These reports are intended to help Canadian companies identify foreign business opportunities and learn more about their target markets. You must register for a (free) password to access many of the DFAIT market reports. Look for your country, choose one of the links to relevant Canadian consulates and embassies in the country, then click on the link to Industry Sector Market Reports and Links. Also at the consulate/embassy level, click on the Market Prospect link for data on business conditions and for advice on doing business in the country.

http://www.infoexport.gc.ca/ie-en/EServices.jsp

5. *Economist.com—Country Briefings* Established in 1946, the Country Briefings are a leading source of country-specific information. Now on the magazine's website, the briefings cover sixty countries with succinct forecasts, economic and political profiles, core statistics, essential recent articles, and in-depth surveys from the *Economist*. Note that only some of the information is free.

http://www.economist.com/countries/

6. *Ernst & Young* EY publishes reports that cover the tax details (and related country information) associated with

doing business in over 130 countries, but finding the information is not straightforward. Click on Global in the top right corner of the EY site, then click on the country. The amount of information on each country varies.

http://www.ey.com/global/content.nsf/International/Home

7. *Industry Canada* (3 links)

Trade and Investment Country reports, prepared by the International Cooperation Directorate, provide a quick overview of business conditions in selected countries where opportunities exist for Canadian firms.

http://www.ic.gc.ca/epic/site/ibi-iai.nsf/en/h_bi18601e.html

Trade Data Online This site offers the ability to generate customized reports on Canadian and U.S. trade with over two hundred countries—by product and by industry.

http://www.ic.gc.ca/epic/site/tdo-dcd.nsf/en/Home

Market Research This site provides Canadian and U.S. resources on international markets. Check for publication dates, as some of these reports are outdated. You can get the newest U.S. reports from the U.S. Department of Commerce site listed above.

http://strategis.gc.ca/epic/site/imr-ri2.nsf/en/gr-01000e.html

8. *International Monetary Fund (IMF) Country Information* The site has Staff Country Reports, press releases, and occasional/working papers on almost every country. If you are quoted a price when you click on something, look for a link to the PDF full-text version—it should be free. The Staff Country Reports are particularly good, but they can be lengthy. Save time by checking the table of contents of the PDF files for the pages with tables and charts.

http://www.imf.org/external/country/index.htm

9. *International Trade Administration (ITA; U.S.)* The ITA page has resources to help U.S. businesses compete globally. These resources include guides to doing business in many countries as well as trade and economic statistics.

This site includes access to the U.S. government's Country Commercial Guides as well as to Market Access and Compliance information for many countries.

http://trade.gov/index.asp

10. *Country Insights* The Canadian Department of Foreign Affairs and International Trade's Centre for Intercultural Learning has created a website with information on more than two hundred countries. It covers social, political, economic, environmental, and cultural issues. The *cultural information* section of this site is particularly noteworthy. It provides commentary by both a national and a Canadian about the culture of each country. The background of each *cultural interpreter* is provided in some detail so that you can gain a deeper understanding of the individual's perspective.

http://www.intercultures.ca/cil-cai/country_insights-en.asp

11. *United Nations Industrial Development Organization (UNIDO): Country Information* The UNIDO offers basic data (on GDP, manufactured exports, manufacturing value added, and so on) for most countries of the world as well as more detailed statistics on items such as labor productivity and wage rates by industry.

http://www.unido.org/index.php?id=4879

12. *World Bank Group: Country Data* Tables drawn from the World Bank Development Indicators give quick reference numbers for 206 countries as well as various regional groupings. This site also includes some links to other useful international agency sites.

http://web.worldbank.org/WBSITE/EXTERNAL/DATA
STATISTICS/0,,contentMDK:20535285~menuPK:11926
94~pagePK:64133150~piPK:64133175~theSitePK:23941
9,00.html

Book Series

Graphic Arts Center Publishing, *Culture Shock Guides.* Often written by expatriates or travelers.

Greenwood Publishing Group, *Culture and Customs Series.* In-depth coverage of a variety of countries, each by different experts, covering history, religion, customs, media, and the arts from a predominantly anthropological perspective.

Interlink Publishing, *In Focus Travel Guides.* As the name implies, but with broader coverage of people, culture, politics, government, economics, religion, and so on.

McGraw-Hill, *Comparative Societies Series.* A series of short books providing material on the society, politics, and economics of countries. The opening chapter of each establishes historical and cultural context, while subsequent chapters focus on the basic institutions, social stratification, social problems, and social change.

Survival Books, *Living and Working in . . .* Series (15 countries) Practical advice for expatriates, retirees, prospective home buyers, and so on.

World Trade Press, *Country Business Guides Series* (12 countries), *Passport to the World Series* (25 countries), and the *Global Road Warrior* (175 countries) all contain useful information.

Notes

CHAPTER I

1. Some vignettes adapted from Cushner, K., & Brislin, R.W. (1996). *Intercultural interactions: A practical guide.* Thousand Oaks, CA: Sage.

2. Our definition of globalization is drawn from our colleague Barbara Parker's work on this topic in *Globalization and Business Practice: Managing across boundaries.* London: Sage, 1999.

3. For insight as to what the dominant culture in the future might be, see Zakaria, F. (2008). *The post-American world.* New York: W.W. Norton.

4. See Ritzer, G. (2008). *The McDonaldization of Society 5.* Thousands Oaks, CA: Pine Forge Press.

5. For more on this topic, see Smith, P.B., & Bond, M.H. (1999). *Social psychology across cultures.* Boston: Allyn and Bacon.

6. For example, see the following: Hofstede, G. (1980) *Culture's consequences: International differences in work-related values.* Beverly Hills, CA: Sage; Schwartz, S.H. (1992). Universals in the content and structure of values: Theoretical advances and empirical tests in 20 countries. In M.P. Zanna

(Ed)., *Advances in experimental social psychology* (pp. 1–65). San Diego: Academic Press.; Trompenaars, F. (1993). *Riding the waves of culture*. Burr Ridge, IL: Irwin.; and Triandis, H. C. (1972). *The analysis of subjective culture*. New York: Wiley.

7. While this concept has gone by various names over the years, including intercultural competence, global mindset, and global competencies, the definition of the idea as a special type of intelligence can be attributed to Chris Earley in his 2002 article Redefining interactions across cultures and organizations: Moving forward with cultural intelligence. *Psychological Bulletin*, 91, pp. 271–299 and in his 2003 book with Soon Ang, *Cultural intelligence: Individual interactions across cultures*. Stanford, CA: Stanford University Press.

8. Recently several approaches to measuring cultural intelligence have been developed. A measure of cultural intelligence as defined in this book has been developed by an international consortium of researchers called The Cultural Intelligence Project.

CHAPTER 2

1. Source: Adapted from Cushner, K., & Brislin, R. W. (1996). *Intercultural interactions: A practical guide*. Thousand Oaks, CA: Sage.

2. See Thomas et al. (2008). Cultural intelligence: Domain and assessment. *International Journal of Cross-Cultural Management*, 8 (2), 123–144.

3. Hofstede, G. (1980) *Culture's consequences: International differences in work-related values*. Beverly Hills, CA: Sage.

4. For an interesting discussion of organizational culture, see Deal, T., & Kennedy, A. (1982). *Corporate culture: The rites and rituals of corporate life*. Reading, MA: Addison-Wesley.

5. For more information on the process of acculturation, see Berry, J. W. (1990). The psychology of acculturation: Understanding individuals moving between cultures. In R. Brislin (Ed.), *Cross-cultural research and methodology series: Vol. 14. Applied cross-cultural psychology* (pp. 232–252). Newbury Park, CA: Sage.

6. Psychologists are just beginning to fully understand

these so-called *bicultural* individuals. For examples of this research, see Benet-Martínez, V., Lee, F., & Leu, J. (2006). Biculturalism and cognitive complexity: Expertise in cultural representations. *Journal of Cross-Cultural Psychology, 37,* 386–407; and Fu, J. H-Y., Chiu, C-Y., Morris, M.W., & Young, M.J. (2007). Spontaneous inferences from cultural cues. Varying responses of cultural insiders and outsiders. *Journal of Cross-Cultural Psychology, 38,* 58–75.

7. Recent research suggests that the development of higher-order cognitive processes may be different depending on how individuals manage their multiple cultural identities. See Brannen, M.Y., Garcia, D., & Thomas, D.C. (2008). The impact of biculturalism on cross-cultural cognitive and behavioral skill sets. Paper presented to the annual meeting of the Academy of Management, Anaheim, CA.

8. The metaphor of an iceberg to represent culture comes from Schein, E.H. (1985). *Organizational culture and leadership.* San Francisco: Jossey-Bass.

9. The idea of tight and loose cultures comes from Pelto, P.J. (1968). The difference between tight and loose societies. *Transaction,* April, 37–40, cited in Triandis, H.C. (1995). *Individualism and collectivism.* Boulder, CO: Westview.

10. For a more complete discussion of convergence versus divergence of culture, see Smith, P.B., & Bond, M.H. (1999). *Social psychology across cultures.* Boston: Allyn and Bacon; and Ralston, D.A., Holt, D.H., Terpstra, R.H., & Yu, K. (1997). The impact of national culture and economic ideology on managerial work values: A study of the United States, Russia, Japan, and China. *Journal of International Business Studies, 28* (1), 177–207.

11. For more on recontextualization, see Brannen, M.Y. (2004). When Mickey loses face: Recontextualization, semantic fit, and the semiotics of foreignness. *Academy of Management Review, 29,* 593–616.

12. Some researchers suggest that we can better describe cultures as being in a states of multiple stable equilibriums because of the interaction of culture with other aspects of the environment. See Cohen (2001). Cultural variation: Considerations and implications. *Psychological Bulletin, 127,* 451–471.

13. The dimensions of individualism and collectivism have been used to explain and predict a diverse array of social behavior. However, some scholars have suggested that they have been overused and that other dimensions have been neglected. For example, see Earley, P.C., & Gibson, C.B. (1998). Taking stock in our progress on individualism-collectivism: 100 years of solidarity and community. *Journal of Management*, 24, 265–304.

14. The method used by Geert Hofstede in his ground-breaking study is not without its critics. See, for example, Roberts, K.H., & Boyacigiller, N.A. (1984). Cross-national organizational research: The grasp of the blind men. In B.M. Staw & L.L. Cummings (Eds.), *Research in organizational behavior* (Vol. 6, pp. 423–475). Greenwich, CT: JAI Press; and Dorfman, P.W., & Howell, J.P. (1988). Dimensions of national culture and effective leadership patterns: Hofstede revisited. *Advances in International Comparative Management*, 3, 127–150.

15. An extensive review of the causes and consequences of individualism and collectivism, including the relationship to affluence, family structure, health, religion, and politics, is contained in Triandis, H.C. (1995). *Individualism and collectivism*. Boulder, CO: Westview.

16. For additional information about these dimensions of culture, how they were derived, and the process of creating the map shown in figure 2.2, see Sagiv, L., & Schwartz, S.H. (1995). Value priorities and readiness for out-group social contact. *Journal of Personality and Social Psychology*, 69, 437–448; Schwartz, S.H. (1992). Universals in the content and structure of values: Theoretical advances and empirical tests in 20 countries. In M.P. Zanna (Ed.), *Advances in Experimental Social Psychology* (pp. 1–65). San Diego: Academic Press; Schwartz, S.H. (1994). Beyond individualism/collectivism: New dimensions of values. In U. Kim, H.C. Triandis, C. Kagitçibasi, S.C. Choi, & G. Yoon (Eds.), *Individualism and collectivism: Theory, applications, and methods* (pp. 85–119). Newbury Park, CA: Sage; and Schwartz, S.H., & Bilsky, W. (1990). Toward a universal psychological structure of human values. *Journal of Personality and Social Psychology*, 53, 550–562.

17. See House et al. (2004). *Culture, leaderships, and organizations: The GLOBE study of 62 societies.* Thousand Oaks, CA: Sage.

18. See Peterson, M.F., & Smith, P.B. (1997). Does national culture or ambient temperature explain cross-cultural differences in role stress? *Academy of Management Journal,* 40, 930–946.

19. GLOBE value scores corrected for social desirability bias as reported in R.J. House et al. (2004). *Culture, leadership, and organizations: The GLOBE study of 62 societies.* Thousand Oaks, CA: Sage.

CHAPTER 3

1. For more information on psychological scripts, see Abelson, R.P. (1981). Psychological status of the script concept. *American Psychologist,* 36, 715–729; Gioa, D.A., & Poole, P.P. (1984). Scripts in organizational behaviour. *Academy of Management Review,* 9, 449–459; and Lord, R.G., & Kernan, M.C. (1987). Scripts as determinants of purposeful behavior in organizations. *Academy of Management Review,* 12, 265–277.

2. Mindfulness is a concept that originated in Zen Buddhism. To learn more about the concept from this perspective, see the writings of the Buddhist monk Thich Nhat Hanh, especially *The miracle of mindfulness* (1999). Boston: Beacon Press; and *Peace is every step: The path of mindfulness in everyday life* (1991). New York: Bantam Books. Mindfulness was introduced into psychology literature by Ellen Langer in her excellent book *Mindfulness* (1989). Cambridge, MA: Perseus Books.

3. The role models that are appropriate vary from culture to culture and are affected by such things as social class and gender. For example, it is much more appropriate for a young U.S. woman to model herself after a business executive than it would be for a Japanese woman to do so, and a tennis player would be a more desirable role model for an upper-class English boy than would a football (soccer) player.

4. The section on how culture affects behavior draws heavily on Thomas, D.C. (2008). *Cross-cultural management: Essential concepts.* Thousand Oaks, CA: Sage.

5. Our approach to treating stereotypes as a natural outcome of social categorization is consistent with classic work on this topic. For example, see Ashmore, R. D., & Del Boca, F. K. (1981). Conceptual approaches to stereotypes and stereotyping. In D. L. Hamilton (Ed.), *Cognitive processes in stereotyping and intergroup behavior* (pp. 1–35). Hillsdale, NJ: Erlbaum.

6. Without wishing in any way to ignore or diminish the dreadful effects of racism in many countries around the world, in this book we assume that our readers do not harbor racist attitudes. That is, they acknowledge differences between groups but do not assume these differences imply superiority or inferiority. They may experience lack of understanding of other cultures and sometimes puzzlement, apprehension, even fear. But they do not feel antagonism, and to the extent that they do, they seek to overcome it. In this book we are assuming that readers have moved beyond the negative attitudes of racism and genuinely seek to manifest their recognition of the equality of all groups and their goodwill toward others in better understanding of these groups and improving relationships with them.

7. *American* is used here to refer to a U.S. person because of common usage. We realize that all people from the Americas are properly referred to as *Americans*.

8. Adapted from Cushner, K., & Brislin, R. W. (1996). *Intercultural interactions: A practical guide*. Thousand Oaks, CA: Sage.

9. For a classic description of what managers do, see Mintzberg, H. (1973). *The nature of managerial work*. New York: Harper & Row.

10. The idea of a repertoire of behaviors as a way to define the behavioral component of cultural intelligence resulted from numerous discussions with members of the International Organizations Network (ION), particularly Allan Bird, Mark Mendenhall, Joyce Osland, Nakiye Boyacigiller, and Schon Beechlor.

11. For more information on these skills see Thomas, D. C., et al. (2008). Cultural intelligence: Domain and assessment. *International Journal of Cross-Cultural Management*, 8 (2), 123–144.

1. For additional information on rational decision making in management and its limitations, see Bazerman, M. (1998). *Judgement in managerial decision making,* 4th Edition. New York: John Wiley & Sons.

2. The problems associated with rational models presented here are based on the concept of bounded rationality. See March, J. G. (1978). Bounded rationality, ambiguity, and the engineering of choice. *Bell Journal of Economics,* 9 (2), 587–608; and March, J., & Simon, H. (1958). *Organizations.* New York: Wiley.

3. See Lindblom, C. (1959). The science of muddling through. *Public Administration Review,* 19, 79–88.

4. The notion of heuristics presented here is derived from a classic article by Amos Tversky and Daniel Kahneman, Judgment under uncertainty: Heuristics and biases. *Science* 185, 1124–1131; and from Nisbett, R. E., & Ross, L. (1980) *Human inference.* Englewood Cliffs, NJ: Prentice-Hall.

5. See March (1978); March & Simon (1958).

6. Maier, N. (1970). *Problem solving and creativity in individuals and groups.* Belmont, CA: Brookes Cole.

7. These motivational biases are based on the effects of differences in the self-concepts of culturally different individuals. See, for example, Erez, M., & Earley, P. C. (1993). *Culture, self-identity, and work.* New York: Oxford University Press.

8. Bontempo, R., Lobel, S. A., & Triandis, H. C. (1990). Compliance and value internalization in Brazil and the U.S.: Effects of allocentrism and anonymity. *Journal of Cross-Cultural Psychology,* 21, 200–213.

9. See, for example, Heine, S. J., & Lehman, D. R. (1995). Cultural variation in unrealistic optimism: Does the West feel more invulnerable than the East? *Journal of Personality and Social Psychology,* 68, 595–607; and Miyamoto, Y., & Ktayama, S. (2002). Cultural variation in correspondence bias: The critical role of attitude diagnosticity and socially constrained behavior. *Journal of Personality and Social Psychology,* 83 (5), 1239–1248.

10. Adapted from a case by Shekshnia, S. V., & Puffer, S. M. (2003). Rus Wane equipment: Joint venture in Russia. In D. C. Thomas (Ed.) *Readings and cases in international*

management: A Cross-cultural perspective. Thousand Oaks: CA: Sage.

11. *Guanxi* is often translated as a network of relationships. It is, however, an indigenous Chinese construct that can only be properly understood within the Chinese context. See, for example, Gold, T., Guthrie, D., & Wank, D. (Eds.) (2002). *Social connections in China: Institutions, culture, and the changing nature of Guanxi*. Cambridge, MA: Cambridge University Press.

12. Shackleton, V., & Newell, S. (1994). European management selection methods: A comparison of five countries. *International Journal of Selection and Assessment, 2*, 91–102.

13. For more information on this central ethical question, see Donaldson, T. (1989). *The ethics of international business*. New York: Oxford University Press.

14. The idea of a set of fundamental human rights that are invariant across cultures is central to moving beyond cultural relativism. See Donaldson (1989), but also Donaldson, T. (1996). Values in tension: Ethics away from home. *Harvard Business Review*, Sept./Oct., 48–62.

CHAPTER 5

1. Some vignettes condensed from cases by Cushner, K., & Brislin, R. W. (1996). *Intercultural interactions: A practical guide*. Thousand Oaks, CA: Sage Publications.

2. The idea of cultural grounding in communication comes from Clark, H.H., & Brennan, S.E. (1991). Grounding in communication. In *Perspectives on Socially Shared Cognition*. Washington, DC: American Psychological Association.

3. Estimates of the number of languages in the world vary between two thousand and ten thousand. However, the number in use by significant numbers of people is many fewer. In many countries there are at least two native languages, and in some cases, such as Papua New Guinea, there are hundreds.

4. The question of the optimal age to learn a foreign language has long been studied. For more information, see Asher, J.J., & Garcia, R. (1969). The optimal age to learn a foreign language. *Modern Language Journal, 53*, 334–341. There is little debate, however, about the fact that children pick up new

languages "naturally" while older learners generally have to struggle long and hard to achieve even moderate fluency.

5. See, for example, Giles, H., Taylor, D.M., & Bourhis, R.Y. (1973). Towards a theory of interpersonal accommodation through speech: Some Canadian data. *Language in Society, 2*, 177–192.

6. See Felson, R.B. (1978). Aggression is impression management. *Social Psychology Quarterly, 41*, 259–281, cited in Smith, P.B., & Bond, M.H. (1999). *Social psychology across cultures*. Boston: Allyn and Bacon.

7. This example taken from an interesting, informative, and humorous look at the English language by Bill Bryson (2001). *The mother tongue: English and how it got that way*. New York: Harper Collins.

8. This list of second-language strategies is adapted from Adler, N.J., & Kiggundu, M.N. (1983). In D. Landis & R. Brislin (Eds.). *Handbook of intercultural training*. Elmsford, NY: Pergamon Press.

9. Engholm, C. (1991). *When business East meets business West: The guide to practice and protocol in the Pacific Rim*. New York: John Wiley.

10. This anecdote was adapted from a case study by Joseph DiStefano (2003). Johannes van den Bosch sends an e-mail. In D.C. Thomas (Ed.), *Readings and cases in international management: A cross-cultural perspective*. Thousand Oaks, CA: Sage.

11. The idea of social distance or, as it is also called, proxemics, is drawn from Hall, E.T. (1966). *The hidden dimension*. Garden City, NY: Doubleday.

12. See, for example, Andersen, P.A., & Bowman, L. (1985). *Positions of power: Nonverbal cues of status and dominance in organizational communication*. Paper presented at the annual convention of the international communication association, Honolulu, HI; and Aronoff, J., Woike, B.A., & Hyman, L.M. (1992).Which are the stimuli in facial displays of anger and happiness? *Journal of Personality and Social Psychology, 62*, 1050–1066.

13. Ekman, P.W. (1982). *Emotion in the human face*, 2nd Edition. Cambridge: Cambridge University Press.

14. Graham, J.L. (1987). A theory of interorganizational negotiations. *Research in Marketing*, 9, 163–183.

15. See Gelfand, M.J., & McCusker, C. (2002). Metaphor and cultural construction of negotiation: A paradigm for research and practice. In M.J. Gannon & K.L. Newman (Eds.), *Handbook of cross-cultural management* (pp. 292–314). Malden, MA: Blackwell.

CHAPTER 6

1. While this is a Western definition of leadership (see Yukl, G. [1994]. *Leadership in organizations*, 3rd Edition. Upper Saddle River, NJ: Prentice-Hall), some international consensus seems to be building toward this definition. See House, R.J., Wright, N.S., & Aditya, R.N. (1997) Cross-cultural research on organizational leadership: A critical analysis and a proposed theory. In P.C. Earley & M. Erez (Eds.), *New Perspectives on international industrial/organizational psychology* (pp. 535–625). San Francisco: New Lexington Press.

2. As appealing as the idea may be, certain characteristics of individuals that are consistently related to leader emergence or leader effectiveness have not been validated by the research. For more on this topic, see Dorfman, P.W. (1996). International and cross-cultural leadership. In J. Punnitt & O. Shenkar (Eds.), *Handbook for international management research* (pp. 276–349). Cambridge, MA: Blackwell

3. See Dorfman (1996).

4. Al-Kubaisy, A. (1985). A model in the administrative development of Arab Gulf countries. *The Arab Gulf,* 17 (2), 29–48.

5. Nakane, C. (1970). *Japanese society.* Berkeley: University of California Press.

6. Drucker, P. (1994). The new superpower: The overseas Chinese. *Wall Street Journal* (December 20), 17.

7. Sorge, A. (1993). Management in France. In D. Hickson (Ed.), *Management in Western Europe: Society, culture and organization in twelve nations* (pp. 65–87). New York: Walter de Gruyter.

8. See Puffer, S.M. (1994). A portrait of Russian business leaders. *Academy of Management Executive,* 8 (1), 41–54;

and Napier, N.K., & Thomas, D.C. (2004). *Managing relationships in transition economies.* New York: Praeger.

9. Management by Objectives (MBO) is a management technique based on the findings of goal-setting theory. For more information on this topic, see Locke, E.A., & Latham, G.P. (1984). *Goal setting: a motivational technique that works.* Englewood Cliffs, NJ: Prentice-Hall; and Erez, M., & Earley, P.C. (1987). Comparative analysis of goal-setting strategies across cultures. *Journal of Applied Psychology, 71,* 658–665.

10. Adapted from an unpublished case by Stanislav V. Shekshnia.

11. For more information on paternalism see Aycan, Z. (2008). Cross-cultural approaches to leadership. In P.B. Smith, M.F. Peterson, & D.C. Thomas (Eds.). *The handbook of cross-cultural management research* (pp. 219–238). Thousand Oaks, CA: Sage.

12. See for example, Casey, C. (1999). Come, join our family: Discipline and integration in corporate organizational cultures. *Human Relations, 52* (2), 155–178.

13. This case is adapted from Shepherd, D. (2003). Common bond values at the New Zealand office of AT&T. In D.C. Thomas (Ed.), *Readings and cases in international management: A cross-cultural perspective* (pp. 92–100). Thousand Oaks, CA: Sage Publications.

14. For more information on transformational leadership, see Bass, B.M. (1985). *Leadership and performance beyond expectations.* New York: Free Press; and Conger, J.A., & Kanungo, R. (1988). *Charismatic leadership: The elusive factor in organizational effectiveness.* San Francisco: Jossey-Bass.

15. For example see House, R.J., Wright, N.S., & Aditya, R.N. (1997). Cross-cultural research on organizational leadership: A critical analysis and a proposed theory. In P.C. Earley & M. Erez (Eds.), *New Perspectives on international industrial/organizational psychology* (pp. 535–625). San Francisco: New Lexington Press.

16. For an example of this effect, see Thomas, D.C., & Ravlin, E.C. (1995). Responses of employees to cultural adaptation by a foreign manager. *Journal of Applied Psychology, 80,* 133–146.

1. For more information on group processes, see Goodman, P. S., Elizabeth, C. R., & Schminke, M. (1987). Understanding groups in organizations. In B. Staw & L. Cummings (Eds.), *Research in organizational behavior* (Vol. 9, pp. 124–128). Greenwich, CT: JAI Press; and Hackman, J. R. (1991). *Groups that work (and those that don't)*. San Francisco: Jossey-Bass.

2. In the Western world, the *hijab* has come to symbolize enforced silence. However, this is not a universal view among Muslim women. Some see it as a woman's assertion that judgment of her physical person is to play no role in social interaction because by wearing it her appearance is not subjected to public scrutiny.

3. See Arrow, H., & McGrath, J. E. (1995). Membership dynamics in groups at work: A theoretical framework. *Research in Organizational Behavior, 17,* 373–411.

4. Janis, I. (1982). *Groupthink.* Boston: Houghton Mifflin.

5. Mullen, B., & Baumeister, R. F. (1987). Groups' effects on self-attention and performance: Social loafing, social facilitation, and social impairment. In C. Hendrick (Ed.), *Review of personality and social psychology* (pp. 189–206). Newbury Park, CA: Sage.

6. This classic experiment is described in Ringelman, M. (1913). Recherches sur les moteurs animes: travails de l'homme. *Annales de l'Institut Nationale Agronomique, 12,* 1–40.

7. Process losses among individualists and collectivists also involve the extent to which the group members believe they are interacting with their in-group. For more on this topic, see Earley, P. C. (1989). Social loafing and collectivism: A comparison of the U.S. and the People's Republic of China. *Administrative Science Quarterly, 34,* 565–581; and Earley, P. C. (1993). East meets West meets Mid-East: Further explorations of collectivistic and individualistic work groups. *Academy of Management Journal, 36,* 319–348.

8. The three avenues of cultural influence on groups is described in more detail in Thomas, D. C., Ravlin, E. C., & Wallace, A. W. (1996). Effect of cultural diversity in work groups. *Research in Sociology of Organizations, 14,* 1–33.

9. For a summary of this research, see Goodman, P. S., Ravlin, E. C., & Argote, L. (1986). Current thinking about

groups: Setting the stage for new ideas. In P.S. Goodman (Ed.), *Designing effective work groups.* San Francisco: Jossey-Bass.

10. Walker, R. (1999) Picnic in Samoa. In N. Monin, J. Monin, & R. Walker (Eds.), *Narratives of business and society: Differing New Zealand voices* (pp. 143–153). Auckland: Longman.

11. Nemeth, C.J. (1992). Minority dissent as a stimulant to group performance. In S. Worchel, W. Wood, & J.A. Simpson (Eds.), *Group process and productivity* (pp. 95–111). Newbury Park, CA: Sage.

12. For a more complete description of the effects of cultural distance, see Thomas, D.C. (2002). *Essentials of international management: A cross-cultural perspective.* Thousand Oaks, CA: Sage.

13. Pearce, J.A., & Ravlin, E.C. (1987). The design and activation of self regulating work groups. *Human Relations,* 11, 751–782.

14. The idea of "mapping" and then "bridging" across cultures is outlined in H.W. Lane, J.J. DiStefano, & M.L. Maznevski. (2000). *International management behavior.* Malden, MA: Blackwell.

15. This case was adapted from Maznevski, M.L., & Chudoba, K.M. (2000). Bridging space over time: Global virtual team dynamics and effectiveness. *Organization Science,* 11 (5), 473–492.

16. For more information on this emerging topic, see an excellent book edited by Cris Gibson & Susan Cohen (2003). *Virtual teams that work: Creating conditions for virtual team effectiveness.* San Francisco: Jossey-Bass.

CHAPTER 8

1. For additional information on the inadequacy of stereotypes and the need to understand them in context, see an excellent article by Joyce Osland and Allan Bird, Beyond sophisticated stereotyping: Cultural sense making in context. In D.C. Thomas (Ed.), (2003). *Readings and cases in international management: A cross-cultural perspective* (pp. 58–70). Thousand Oaks, CA: Sage.

2. This diagram is adapted from an idea first presented

in Vijay Govindarajan and Anil Gupta's excellent book on global strategy, *The quest for global dominance* (2001). San Francisco: Jossey-Bass.

3. The concept of social learning was introduced by Albert Bandura. For a more extensive discussion, see Bandura, A. (1977). *Social learning theory*. Englewood Cliffs, NJ: Prentice-Hall.

4. Adapted from a case by Govindarajan & Gupta (2001: 126) and from the experiences of our colleague Mary Yoko Brannen.

5. Adapted from a case in Napier & Thomas (2004).

6. The idea that all expatriates go through a U-curve of adjustment was first presented in Lysgaard, S. (1955). Adjustment in a foreign society: Norwegian Fulbright grantees visiting the United States. *International Social Science Bulletin,* 7, 45–51; and Gullahorn, J.T., & Gullahorn, J.E. (1963). An extension of the U-curve hypothesis. *Journal of Social Issues,* 19, 33–47. However, recent research has suggested that this pattern of adjustment may be far from universal. See Black, J.S., & Mendenhall, M. (1991). The U-curve adjustment hypothesis revisited: A review and theoretical framework. *Journal of International Business Studies,* 22 (2), 225–247.

7. The phrase "very difficult" is classic Japanese understatement. New Zealanders would say "a bit of a worry" to express the same sentiment.

8. This case adapted from Inkson, K., and Myers, B. (2003). "The big O.E.": International travel and career development. *Career Development International,* 8 (4), 170–181.

CONCLUSION

1. This simple quiz is not diagnostic. That is, it can't *predict* how effective you will be at interacting across cultures. The actual measurement of cultural intelligence requires a sophisticated set of assessment tools. For more information about assessing cultural intelligence contact the Cultural Intelligence Project at cqstudy@sfu.ca.

APPENDIX I

1. Adapted from Kuhn & McPartland (1954).

Bibliography

Abelson, R.P. (1981). Psychological status of the script concept. *American Psychologist, 36,* 715–729.

Adler, N.J., & Kiggundu, M.N. (1983). Awareness at the crossroad: Designing translator-based training programs. In D. Landis & R. Brislin (Eds.). *Handbook of intercultural training.* Elmsford, NY: Pergamon Press.

Al-Kubaisy, A. (1985). A model in the administrative development of Arab Gulf countries. *The Arab Gulf,* 17 (2), 29–48.

Andersen, P.A., & Bowman, L. (1985). *Positions of power: Nonverbal cues of status and dominance in organizational communication.* Paper presented at the annual convention of the International Communication Association, Honolulu, HI.

Aronoff, J., Woike, B.A., & Hyman, L.M. (1992). Which are the stimuli in facial displays of anger and happiness? *Journal of Personality and Social Psychology,* 62, 1050–1066.

Arrow, H., & McGrath, J.E. (1993). Membership matters: How member change and continuity affect small group structure, process, and performance. *Small Group Research,* 24, 334–361.

Asher, J.J., & Garcia, R. (1969). The optimal age to learn a foreign language. *Modern Language Journal, 53,* 334–341.

Ashmore, R.D., & Del Boca, F.K. (1981). Conceptual approaches to stereotypes and stereotyping. In D.L. Hamilton (Ed.), *Cognitive processes in stereotyping and intergroup behavior* (pp. 1–35). Hillsdale, NJ: Erlbaum.

Aycan, Z. (2008). Cross-cultural approaches to leadership. In P.B. Smith, M.F. Peterson, & D.C. Thomas (Eds.) *Handbook of cross-cultural management research* (pp. 219-238). Thousand Oaks, CA: Sage.

Bandura, A. (1977). *Social learning theory.* Englewood Cliffs, NJ: Prentice-Hall.

Bartlett, C.A., & Ghoshal, S. (1989). *Managing across borders: The transnational solution.* Boston: Harvard Business School Press.

Bass, B.M. (1985). *Leadership and performance beyond expectation.* New York: Free Press.

Bazerman, M. (1998). *Judgement in managerial decision making,* 4th Edition. New York: John Wiley & Sons.

Berry, J.W. (1990). The psychology of acculturation: Understanding individuals moving between cultures. In R. Brislin (Ed.), *Cross-cultural research and methodology series: Vol. 14. Applied cross-cultural psychology* (pp. 232–252). Newbury Park, CA: Sage.

Black, J.S., & Mendenhall, M. (1991). The U-curve adjustment hypothesis revisited: A review and theoretical framework. *Journal of International Business Studies, 22,* 225–247.

Bontempo, R., Lobel, S.A., & Triandis, H.C. (1990). Compliance and value internalization in Brazil and the U.S.: Effects of allocentrism and anonymity. *Journal of Cross-Cultural Psychology, 21,* 200–213.

Brannen, M.Y. (2004). When Mickey loses face: Recontextualization, semantic fit, and the semiotics of foreignness. *Academy of Management Review, 29* (4), 593–616.

Brannen, M.Y., Garcia, D., & Thomas, D.C. (2008). *The impact of biculturalism on cross-cultural cognitive and behavioral skills.* Paper presented to the annual Meeting of the Academy of Management, Anaheim, CA.

Bryson, B. (2001). *The mother tongue: English and how it got that way.* New York: HarperCollins.

Casey, C. (1999). Come join our family: Discipline and integration in corporate organization cultures. *Human Relations, 52* (2), 155–178.

Catlin, L.B., & White, T.F. (2001). *International business: Cultural sourcebook and case studies.* Cincinnati, OH: South-Western College Publishing.

Clark, H.H., & Brennan, S.E. (1991). Grounding in communication. *Perspectives on Socially Shared Communication,* Washington, DC: American Psychological Association.

Cohen, D. (2001). Cultural variation: Consideration and implications. *Psychological Bulletin, 127,* 451–471.

Conger, J.A., & Kanungo, R. (1988). *Charismatic leadership: The elusive factor in organizational effectiveness.* San Francisco: Jossey-Bass.

Cushner, K., & Brislin, R.W. (1996). *Intercultural interactions: A practical guide.* Thousand Oaks, CA: Sage

Deal, T., & Kennedy, A. (1982). *Corporate culture: The rites and rituals of corporate life.* Reading, MA: Addison-Wesley.

DiStefano, J. (2003). Johannes Bosch sends an e-mail. In D.C. Thomas (Ed.). *Readings and cases in international management: A cross-cultural perspective* (pp. 347–350). Thousand Oaks, CA: Sage Publications.

Donaldson, T. (1989). *The ethics of international business.* New York: Oxford University Press.

———. (1996). Values in tension: Ethics away from home. *Harvard Business Review,* Sept./Oct., 48–62.

Dorfman, P.W. (1996). International and cross-cultural leadership. In B.J. Punnitt & O. Shenkar (Eds.), *Handbook for international management research* (pp. 276–349). Cambridge, MA: Blackwell.

Dorfman, P.W., & Howell, J.P. (1988). Dimensions of national culture and effective leadership patterns: Hofstede revisited. *Advances in international comparative management, 3,* 127–150.

Drucker, P. (1994). The new superpower: The overseas Chinese. *Wall Street Journal* (December 20), 17.

Earley, P.C. (1989). Social loafing and collectivism: A comparison of the U.S. and the People's Republic of China. *Administrative Science Quarterly, 34,* 565–581.

————. (1993). East meets West meets Mid-East: Further explorations of collectivistic and individualistic work groups. *Academy of Management Journal*, 36, 319–348.

————. (2002). Redefining interactions across cultures and organizations: Moving forward with cultural intelligence. *Research in Organizational Behavior*, 24, 271–299.

Earley, P.C., & Ang, S. (2003). *Cultural intelligence: Individual interactions across cultures*. Stanford, CA: Stanford University Press.

Earley, P.C., & Gibson. C.B. (1998). Taking stock in our progress on individualism-collectivism: 100 years of solidarity and community. *Journal of Management*, 24, 265–304.

Ekman, P.W. (1982). *Emotion in the human face*, 2nd Edition. Cambridge: Cambridge University Press.

Engholm, C. (1991). *When business East meets business West: The guide to practice and protocol in the Pacific rim*. New York: Wiley.

Erez, M., & Earley, P.C. (1987). Comparative analysis of goal-setting strategies across cultures. *Journal of Applied Psychology*, 71, 658–665.

————. (1993). *Culture, self-identity, and work*. New York: Oxford University Press.

Felson, R.B. (1978). Aggression is impression management. *Social Psychology Quarterly*, 41, 259–281.

Fu, J. H-Y., Chiu, C-Y., Morris, M.W., & Young, M.J. (2007). Spontaneous inferences from cultural cues. Varying responses of cultural insiders and outsiders. *Journal of Cross-Cultural Psychology*, 38, 58–75.

Gelfand, M.J., & McCusker, C. (2002). Metaphor and cultural construction of negotiation: A paradigm for research and practice. In M.J. Gannon & K.L. Newman (Eds.), *Handbook of cross-cultural management* (pp. 292–314). Malden, MA: Blackwell.

Gibson, C.B., & Cohen, S.G. (Eds.) (2003). *Virtual teams that work: Creating conditions for virtual team effectiveness*. San Francisco: Jossey-Bass.

Giles, H., Taylor, D.M., & Bourhis, R.Y. (1973). Towards a theory of interpersonal accommodation through speech: Some Canadian data. *Language in Society*, 2, 177–192.

Gioa, D.A., & Poole, P.P. (1984). Scripts in organizational behaviour. *Academy of Management Review, 9,* 449–459

Gold, T., Guthrie, D., & Wank, D. (Eds.) (2002). *Social connections in China: Institutions, culture, and the changing nature of Guanxi.* Cambridge: Cambridge University Press.

Goodman, P.S., Ravlin, E.C., & Argote, L. (1986). Current thinking about groups: Setting the stage for new ideas. In P.S. Goodman (Ed.), *Designing effective work groups.* San Francisco: Jossey-Bass.

Goodman, P.S., Ravlin, E.C., & Schminke, M. (1987). Understanding groups in organizations. In B. Staw & L. Cummings (Eds.), *Research in organizational behaviour* (Vol. 9, pp. 124–128). Greenwich, CT: JAI Press.

Govindarajan, V., & Gupta, A.K. (2001). *The quest for global dominance.* San Francisco: Jossey-Bass.

Graham, J.L. (1987). A theory of interorganizational negotiations. *Research in Marketing, 9,* 163–183.

Gullahorn, J.T., & Gullahorn, J.E. (1963). An extension of the U-curve hypothesis. *Journal of Social Issues, 19,* 33–47.

Hackman, J.R. (1991). *Groups that work (and those that don't).* San Francisco: Jossey-Bass.

Hall, E.T. (1966). *The hidden dimension.* Garden City, NY: Doubleday.

Heine, S.J., & Lehman, D.R. (1995). Cultural variation in unrealistic optimism: Does the West feel more invulnerable than the East? *Journal of Personality and Social Psychology, 68,* 595–607.

Hofstede, G. (1980) *Culture's consequences: International differences in work-related values.* Beverly Hills, CA: Sage.

House, R.J., Hanges, P.J., Javidan, M., Dorfman, P.W., & Gupta, V. (2004). *Culture, leadership, and organizations: The GLOBE study of 62 societies.* Thousand Oaks, CA: Sage.

House, R.J., Wright, N.S., & Aditya, R.N. (1997). Cross-cultural research on organizational leadership: A critical analysis and a proposed theory. In P.C. Earley & M. Erez (Eds.), *New Perspectives on international industrial/organizational psychology* (pp. 535–625). San Francisco: New Lexington Press.

Inkson K., and Myers, B. (2003). "The big O.E.": International travel and career development. *Career Development International*, 8 (4), 170–181.

Janis, I. L. (1982). *Groupthink*. Boston: Houghton Mifflin.

Kuhn, M. H., & McPartland, T. S. (1954). An empirical investigation of self-attitudes. *American Sociological Review*, 19 (1), 68–76.

Lane, H. W., DiStefano, J. J., & Maznevski, M. L. (2000). *International management behavior: Text, readings and cases*. Malden, MA: Blackwell.

Langer, E. J. (1989). *Mindfulness*. Cambridge, MA: Perseus Books.

Lindblom, C. (1959). The science of muddling through. *Public Administration Review*, 19 (2), 278–294.

Locke, E. A., & Latham, G. P. (1984). *Goal setting: a motivational technique that works*. Englewood Cliffs, NJ: Prentice-Hall.

Lord, R. G., & Kernan, M. C. (1987). Scripts as determinants of purposeful behavior in organizations. *Academy of Management Review*, 12, 265–277.

Lysgaard, S. (1955). Adjustment in a foreign society: Norwegian Fulbright grantees visiting the United States. *International Social Science Bulletin*, 7, 45–51.

Maier, N. (1970). *Problem solving and creativity in individuals and groups*. Belmont, CA: Brookes/Cole.

March, J. G. (1978). Bounded rationality, ambiguity, and the engineering of choice. *Bell Journal of Economics*, 9 (2), 587–608.

March, J., & Simon, H. (1958). *Organizations*. New York: Wiley.

Maznevski, M. L., & Chudoba, K. M. (2000). Bridging space over time: Global virtual team dynamics and effectiveness. *Organization Science*, 11 (5), 473–492.

McLuhan, M. (1962). *The Gutenberg galaxy*. Toronto: University of Toronto Press.

———. (1964). *Understanding media: the extensions of man*. New York: McGraw-Hill.

Mendenhall, M., Lane, H., Maznevski, M., & McNett, J. (Eds.) (2003). *Handbook of cross-cultural management*. Oxford: Blackwell.

Miyamoto, Y., & Ktayama, S. (2002). Cultural variation in correspondence bias: The critical role of attitude diagnosticity and socially constrained behaviour. *Journal of Personality and Social Psychology*, 83 (5), 1239–1248.

Mullen, B., & Baumeister R. F. (1987). Groups' effects on self-attention and performance: Social loafing, social facilitation, and social impairment. In C. Hendrick (Ed.), *Review of personality and social psychology* (pp. 189–206). Newbury Park, CA: Sage.

Nakane, C. (1970). *Japanese society.* Berkeley: University of California Press.

Napier, N. K., & Thomas, D. C. (2004). *Managing relationships in transition economies.* New York: Praeger.

Nemeth, C. J. (1992). Minority dissent as a stimulant to group performance. In S. Worchel, W. Wood, & J. A. Simpson (Eds.), *Group process and productivity* (pp. 95–111). Newbury Park, CA: Sage.

The New Webster Encyclopedic Dictionary of the English Language. (1971). Chicago: Consolidated Book Publishers.

Nhat Hahn, Thich. (1991). *Peace is every step: The path of mindfulness in everyday life.* New York: Bantam Books.

———. (1999). *The miracle of mindfulness.* Boston: Beacon Press.

Nisbett, R. E., & Ross, L. (1980). *Human inference.* Englewood Cliffs, NJ: Prentice-Hall.

Osland, J., & Bird, A. (2003). Beyond sophisticated stereotyping: Cultural sensemaking in context. In D. C. Thomas (Ed.), *Readings and cases in international management: A cross-cultural perspective* (pp. 58–70). Thousand Oaks: CA: Sage Publications.

Parker, B. (1998). *Globalization: Managing across boundaries.* London: Sage.

Pearce, J. A., & Ravlin, E. C. (1987). The design and activation of self-regulating work groups. *Human Relations*, 11, 751–782.

Pelto, P. J. (1968). The difference between tight and loose societies. *Transaction*, April, 37–40.

Peterson, M. F., & Smith, P. B. (1997). Does national culture or ambient temperature explain cross-cultural differences in role stress? *Academy of Management Journal*, 40, 930–946.

Puffer, S.M. (1994). A portrait of Russian business leaders. *Academy of Management Executive*, 8 (1), 41–54.

Ralston, D.A., Holt, D.H., Terpstra, R.H., & Yu, K. (1997). The impact of national culture and economic ideology on managerial work values: A study of the United States, Russia, Japan, and China. *Journal of International Business Studies*, 28 (1), 177–207.

Ringelman, M. (1913). Recherches sur les moteurs animes: travails de l'homme. *Annales de l'Institut Nationale Agronomique*, 12, 1–40.

Ritzer, G. (2008). *The McDonaldization of Society 5*, Thousand Oaks, CA: Pine Forge Press.

Roberts, K.H., & Boyacigiller, N.A. (1984). Cross-national organizational research: The grasp of the blind men. In B.M. Staw & L.L. Cummings (Eds.), *Research in organizational behavior* (Vol. 6, pp. 423–475). Greenwich, CT: JAI Press.

Sagiv, L., & Schwartz, S.H. (1995). Value priorities and readiness for outgroup social contact. *Journal of Personality and Social Psychology*, 69, 437–448.

Schein, E.H. (1985). *Organizational culture and leadership*. San Francisco: Jossey-Bass.

Schwartz, S.H. (1992). Universals in the content and structure of values: Theoretical advances and empirical tests in 20 countries. In M.P. Zanna (Ed.), *Advances in Experimental Social Psychology* (pp. 1–65). San Diego: Academic Press.

———. (1994). Beyond individualism/collectivism: New dimensions of values. In U. Kim, H.C. Triandis, C. Kagitçibasi, S.C. Choi, & G. Yoon (Eds.), *Individualism and collectivism: Theory, applications, and methods* (pp. 85–119). Newbury Park, CA: Sage.

Schwartz, S.H., & Bilsky, W. (1990). Toward a universal psychological structure of human values. *Journal of Personality and Social Psychology*, 53, 550–562.

Shackleton, V., & Newell, S. (1994). European management selection methods: A comparison of five countries. *International Journal of Selection and Assessment*, 2, 91–102.

Shekshnia, S.V., & Puffer, S.M. (2003). Rus Wane equipment: Joint Venture in Russia. In D.C. Thomas (Ed.), *Readings and cases in international management: A cross-cultural perspective* (pp. 254–266). Thousand Oaks, CA: Sage Publications.

Shepherd, D. (2003). Common bond values at the New Zealand office of AT&T. In D. C. Thomas (Ed.), *Readings and cases in international management: A cross-cultural perspective* (pp. 92–100). Thousand Oaks, CA: Sage Publications.

Smith, P. B., & Bond, M. H. (1999). *Social psychology across cultures*. Boston: Allyn and Bacon.

Sorge, A. (1993). Management in France. In D. Hickson (Ed.), *Management in Western Europe: Society, culture and organization in twelve nations* (pp. 65–87). New York: Walter de Gruyter.

Thomas, D. C. (1998). The expatriate experience: A critical review and synthesis. *Advances in International Comparative Management*, 12, 237–273.

————. (Ed.). (2003) *Readings and cases in international management: A cross-cultural perspective*. Thousand Oaks, CA: Sage.

————. (2008). *Cross-cultural management: Essential concepts*. Thousand Oaks, CA: Sage.

Thomas, D. C., Au, K., & Ravlin, E. C. (2003). Cultural variation and the psychological contract. *Journal of Organizational Behavior*, 24, 451–471.

Thomas, D. C., & Ravlin, E. C. (1995). Responses of employees to cultural adaptation by a foreign manager. *Journal of Applied Psychology*, 80, 133–146.

Thomas, D. C., Ravlin, E. C., & Wallace, A. W. (1996). Effect of cultural diversity in work groups. *Research in Sociology of Organizations*, 14, 1–33.

Thomas, D. C., Stahl, G., Ravlin, E. C., Pekerti, A., Poelmans, S., Maznevski, M., Lazarova, M., Elron, E., Ekelund, B. Z., Cerdin, J.-L., Brislin, R., Aycan, Z., & Au, K. (2006). Cultural intelligence: Domain and assessment. *International Journal of Cross-Cultural Management*, 8 (2), 123–143.

Triandis, H. C. (1972). *The analysis of subjective culture*. New York: Wiley.

————. (1995). *Individualism and collectivism*. Boulder, CO: Westview.

Trompenaars, F. (1993). *Riding the waves of culture*. Burr Ridge, IL: Irwin.

Tuckman, B.W. (1965). Developmental sequence in small groups. *Psychological Bulletin*, 63 (6), 384–399.

Tversky, A., & Kahneman, D. (1980). Judgement under uncertainty: Heuristics and biases, *Science*, 85, 1124–1131.

Walker, R. (1999). Picnic in Samoa. In N. Monin, J. Monin, & R. Walker (Eds.), *Narratives of business and society: Differing New Zealand voices* (pp. 143–153). Auckland: Longman.

Yukl, G. (1994). *Leadership in organizations*, 3rd Edition. Upper Saddle River, NJ: Prentice-Hall.

Zakaria, F. (2008). *The post-American world*. New York: W. W. Norton.

Index

Foreign experience and expatriate assignments, 15, 163–170, 178. *See also* International travel

France
  leadership in, 115
  social behavior in, 58–59, 97
French behavior, understanding, 157–158
Future orientation, 37, 40

Gandhi, Mohandas, 124
Gender, as indicator of group membership, 51
Gender egalitarianism, 37, 40
Germany, bureaucratic negotiation in, 103
Gestures, 98
Global and national culture, 28–30
Global Leadership and Organizational Behaviour Effectiveness (GLOBE) study, 37–41
Global village, 5
Globalization, ix, 5–7, 19, 82, 146, 174
  forces of, 7–8
  of people, 8–11
Great Man theory, 111
Greece, nonverbal communication in, 94–96
Group management
  culturally intelligent, 142–145
  management support, 143
  managing the group environment, 142–144
  rewards, 143
Group status, 143
Groups. *See also* Organizations; Work groups
  cross-cultural social and interest, 159–160

Groupthink, 137, 138
Guanxi, 75

Harmony, 35
Heuristics, 69, 70
Hierarchy, 35
Hofstede, Geert, 23, 34
Home, cross-cultural interactions at, 160–163
Hong Kong and cultural convergence, 30
Human nature, 23–24
Human rights, fundamental, 82–83. *See also* Ethics in decision making
Humane orientation, 37, 40

Implicit communication, 92–93
In-group collectivism, 37, 40
In-groups, 39, 51, 53. *See also* Out-groups
India, nonverbal behavior in, 96
Individualism, 33–34. *See also* Collectivism
  as basis for cultural generalizations, 126
  as characteristic of Westerners, 130
  in communication conventions, 92
  as influential in teams, 138
Individualist cultures
  characteristics of, 33
  decision making in, 71, 73–74, 76
  direct communication convention in, 92–93
  group members in, 131
  groupthink in, 138
  leadership behavior in, 119
  motivation in, 110
  rewards in, 143
  selective perception in, 50

Transformational leadership,
124–125
Translators, 89

Uncertainty
  avoidance of, 37, 40
  tolerance for, 60
United States. *See also* American culture; Americans
  characteristics of leaders in, 109
  cultural imperialism, 13, 29
  cultural profile, 40
  as culturally similar to
    Canada, 81
  as example of individualism,
    72, 73
  example of social behavior
    in, 53
  as loose culture, 29
  as similar to Japan on mastery,
    36
  touching behavior, 97

Value dimensions across
    nations, 35–36
Values, 27
  in communication, 92
  cultural, 23–24, 29–34, 72,
    125, 126
  culture as an organized system
    of, 27
  dimensions of variation in, 31–
    32, 35–36
  historical basis of, 155

as invisible element of culture,
    29
  in multicultural teams, 134
  as part of the cultural field, 88
  as relative to society, 81
  as underlying decision-making
    behavior, 82–83
  as way to anticipate differences, 104

Western culture
  criteria for selection, 75
  model of management, 65
Woods, Tiger, 60–61
Work groups and teams, multicultural, 57, 129–131, 149–
    150, 159–160, 178. *See also*
    Group management
  the challenge of, 131–134
  cultural distance in, 139,
    141–142
  cultural diversity in, 139–141
    developing, 144
  cultural intelligence in, 133
    developing, 135, 145
  group process and performance, 136–139
  making them more effective,
    148–149
  omnipresence, 134–135
  task *vs.* process activities,
    132–133
  types of, 135–136
  virtual multicultural, 145–148

About the Authors

DAVID C. (DAVE) THOMAS is Professor of International Management and Director of the Centre for Global Workforce Strategy at Simon Fraser University, Vancouver, Canada. He also currently serves as Director of the PhD program in business administration.

He is the author of seven books, including *Cross-Cultural Management: Essential Concepts*, from Sage Publications. In addition, he has recently edited (with Peter B. Smith and Mark Peterson) *The Handbook of Cross-Cultural Management Research*, also from Sage Publications. His research on cross-cultural interactions in organizational settings has taken him around the world, and articles based on that research have appeared in numerous journals. His previous academic postings have included positions in New Zealand, Hong Kong, France, and the United States. In addition to teaching at both the undergraduate and postgraduate levels, Dave has developed executive education programs in Australia, New Zealand, Canada, and the United States and has served as a consultant to a number of multinational firms and government agencies in New Zealand and Canada. When not writing or teaching, he can often be found scraping or varnishing (or sometimes sailing) his 1972 Cheoy Lee ketch, *Pounamu*.

KERR INKSON is an Adjunct Professor at the University of Waikato, New Zealand, and an Honorary Professor at Excelerator: The New Zealand Leadership Institute at the University of Auckland, New Zealand. He is the author or coauthor of fourteen books, including *Understanding Careers: The Metaphors of Working Lives, Management: New Zealand Perspectives*, and *The New Careers*. His research in recent years has focused mainly on careers, including international careers; it has involved substantial international travel and has led to articles in numerous academic journals and books. He has held academic positions in New Zealand, the United Kingdom, and the United States, has served as a professor of management at five of New Zealand's universities, and has extensive experience in consulting and executive education, including a term as director of an Executive MBA program. Kerr is semiretired, lives in Auckland, and is active in amateur drama, where his recent roles have included Otto Frank in *The Diary of Anne Frank*, Edward Barrett in *The Barretts of Wimpole Street*, and Lingk in *Glengarry Glenross*.

 **Berrett–Koehler**
Publishers

A community dedicated to creating
a world that works for all

Visit Our Website: www.bkconnection.com

Read book excerpts, see author videos and Internet movies, read
our authors' blogs, join discussion groups, download book apps, find
out about the BK Affiliate Network, browse subject-area libraries of
books, get special discounts, and more!

Subscribe to Our Free E-Newsletter, the *BK Communiqué*

Be the first to hear about new publications, special discount offers,
exclusive articles, news about bestsellers, and more! Get on the list
for our free e-newsletter by going to **www.bkconnection.com**.

Get Quantity Discounts

Berrett-Koehler books are available at quantity discounts for orders
of ten or more copies. Please call us toll-free at (800) 929-2929 or
email us at bkp.orders@aidcvt.com.

Join the BK Community

BKcommunity.com is a virtual meeting place where people from
around the world can engage with kindred spirits to create a world
that works for all. BKcommunity.com members may create their own
profiles, blog, start and participate in forums and discussion groups,
post photos and videos, answer surveys, announce and register for
upcoming events, and chat with others online in real time. Please join
the conversation!